ME, MYSELF, AND WHY?

THE SECRETS TO NAVIGATING CHANGE

Lisa A. Mininni

ME, MYSELF, AND WHY?
THE SECRETS TO NAVIGATING CHANGE

Lisa A. Mininni

PM PUBLISHING, LLC
CANTON, MICHIGAN
www.memyselfandwhy.com

First published by PM Publishing, LLC
Canton, MI 2007

ISBN: 978-0-9792726-0-8

www.memyselfandwhy.com

Printed in the United States of America
Saline, Michigan

This book is dedicated to my husband:

A friend, who keeps me grounded;
A champion, who keeps me going;
A generous spirit, with whom I am free to be me.

ME, MYSELF, AND WHY?
THE SECRETS TO NAVIGATING CHANGE

ACKNOWLEDGMENTS

With Warmest Thanks:

To all my friends who encouraged me in both the good times and the challenging times.

To my book reviewers who took the time and effort to give their insights and suggestions. Thank you Pat, Elena, Carol, Lynn, Jay, Laura, and Dave.

To my manuscript advisor, Virginia Bailey Parker, for your natural talent of seeing what could be even better.

To my book cover designer, Michael at Alpha Advertising, Jennifer at Redwood Photography, and Mathew Dame at Absolute Communications, Inc. (www.absolutecomm.com).

To my former and current clients who have been inspirations, embraced change and lassoed life. To Kristi and Lesley for sharing life's experiences.

To my family, for your support, love, and encouragement as I navigated through my own life changes.

FOREWORD

Some people thrive on change; most people don't because the process of dealing with change—transition—is often fraught with indecision and anxiety. This in-between stage of what was and what will be can take on a troublesome life of its own as a confusing cloud of ambiguity starts to envelop us. This can become so overwhelming that we feel stuck. We don't know which way to turn, or what decision to make next.

Me, Myself, and Why? The Secrets to Navigating Change will take you on a journey along which you will develop insights and tools to navigate through your own personal and professional transitions. In the three sections of the book, you will learn how to master techniques to help you discover who you are and where you want or need to go.

Each one of us has a special *it*, that special talent that is natural to who we are. That special *it* has navigated us in life. However, there are times when our *it* gets misunderstood, ignored or lost. Sometimes a significant illness, downturn in business, job loss, loss of a family member, or seeds of discontentment stops us in our tracks. We feel enveloped in a thick fog or stuck at a crossroads, puzzled about why it is so difficult for us to choose to move on.

Me, Myself, and Why? The Secrets to Navigating Change leads you through the journey of self, where questions are posed, and where you begin to have a realization of that which motivates you, that which makes you unique, that which makes you empowered to live the life you want and that which you were designed to live.

This book is organized into three phases to mirror your steps in your journey to self discovery. In Phase One, *Understanding What Motivates You*, you will begin this journey by reading the stories of others who have gone before you. Each character illustrates a unique way of driving through—or staying stuck—in their Cloud of Ambiguity. Some may even be unaware of those very features that help or hinder them to move ahead through change into transformation. Consider yourself as you read through their stories because you will undoubtedly see elements of yourself in one of more of these characters.

Phase Two, *Finding Possibilities* shifts the focus on what can be. Once you uncover new ways of thinking about what makes up the self in *Myself*, you learn to manage your natural motivators, discover your natural talents, and begin to explore ideas you may not have considered. Each chapter ends with "Self-Reflection Moments" a tool designed to help you apply new ways of thinking about your life, relationships and career.

Phase Three, *Creating New Paths*, focuses on the *Why?* You will learn the secrets to move beyond your Cloud of Ambiguity and begin to take action on that which is important to you. This section can help the way you navigate change and walks with you as you create your vision for your future and a deeper understanding of your purpose.

Enjoy the voyage into the land of *Me, Myself, and Why?* Discover the secrets to finding your passage to your purpose.

PHASE 1:

UNDERSTANDING WHAT MOTIVATES YOU

CHAPTER ONE

IT TOOK A TIRE IRON

On a cold December day, I drove down the road with a million thoughts spinning in my head. I questioned if I was on the right path with starting a business and if writing a book was a good idea since I felt nothing extraordinary has happened in my life. Within a split second though, my thoughts scattered. That was all the time I had to react when I suddenly realized that an object was hurdling with lightning speed straight toward my windshield. I instinctively crossed my arms in front of my face waiting for the pain. While protecting my eyes, my other senses took over. I heard a whooshing sound and metal dinging around in the front seat of my car—but, surprisingly, not the pain I anticipated.

The impact occurred in a fraction of a second, but it seemed as though everything happened in slow motion. I forced one eye open and nervously peeked over my arms, which were still shielding my face. I saw a four-foot, five pound metal bar stretching from my dash board to the passenger's seat.

With a shattered, softball-sized hole in the windshield and shards of glass sprinkled from head to toe, I quickly drove to the side of the road repeatedly saying, "I'm okay, I'm *okay*, *I'm* Okay." My first instinct was to call my appointment to let her know that I'd be late. Of course that was the professional thing to do. I left a message on her voicemail but don't really remember the exact message, although she confirmed later that it was calmly stated— quite different than I was actually feeling.

Semi-trucks continued to whirl by at speeds above 70 mph when the thought occurred to me that I might want to see if I'd been cut by all of the shards of glass. I looked in the mirror, saw no blood, so I must be *okay*. Cautious about further debris popping up from the road, I put the car in drive and slowly crept from the freeway to the first exit and landed in a parking lot. "I'm okay," I kept saying out loud, as if I could convince myself by repeating it.

Eventually, I called my loved one's, repeating to each of them, "I'm okay, I'm okay." I could hardly summon up coherent words as I began telling my husband that a metal bar…a big metal bar…went through my windshield. After assuring him I was "okay," he left work to pick me up. At some point, I called the police and waited for them to arrive. When I thought my knees would support me, I slowly arose out of the car with shards of glass dripping from my hair and winter coat. That's when I saw the damage to the car's hood. The tire iron had impaled the hood and sliced a six-inch gash down to the engine like a hot knife on butter, and then proceeded through the windshield. Upon examination of the tire iron's trajectory, had it not hit the hood, I would have tasted metal. Three officers at different times appeared, saying, "Ma'm you must be on this earth for a reason." "Your mission is not yet complete." "Wow, you were really lucky." I've noticed in my life that the answer to life's tough questions usually comes in a series of threes. I received the confirmation in those three messengers!

Was it luck or some higher power looking out for me? Little did the officers know that I had faced my own mortality years earlier. But…I'm okay. In the end, the windshield needed to be replaced, the dashboard had to be re-sanded and dyed because the shards of glass completely scraped the top dashboard. I, on the other hand, walked away without a scratch.

A little earlier, I asked if starting a business and writing a book was what I should be doing…message received! How did I make the connection between a tire iron hurdling through my windshield and if I was on the right path? The two seem at odds with each other. I suppose it wasn't the tire iron, but the three people who said I was on this earth for a reason.

SELF-REFLECTION MOMENT

How often do you need to hear something before you take a leap?

What experience has left you with questions?

How often do you ask why but don't seek to understand that you are where you need to be at the time for a reason?

Chapter Two

Weathering the Storm

Whether a tire iron is thrown into your way or there have been a series of paths taken, it is human nature to seek clarity when unexpected change occurs. Transition and life's events can be like storms. When it starts to rain, you put on the windshield wipers. When there is a smudge on your glasses, you grab a towel. We seek clarity through these transitional or life events much like we do when it rains.

But in the hot sun of July just ten years before the tire iron experience, I discovered that even through the glow of the summer sun, things were not as clear as I thought. This storm, this life event, would be different and clarity about my life's mission would come years later.

I knew there would be news that I didn't want to hear, I wasn't prepared to hear, but would become the most powerful whirlwind of change. It would spark an innate resilience leading to a wisdom that lay buried beneath. This swift life experience would come in the form of cancer.

At times in our life, we think we're prepared for anything and continue to move on without asking, reflecting or trying to gain a new perspective and, then, an event makes us pause. I thought I was prepared for anything, yet having cancer put me on a path where I would make incremental personal changes. Another pause came in the form of a tire iron ten years later.

Pauses can help us take on new perspectives that, in turn, can lead to powerful revelations. Revelations can change the way you do things and relate to people. But sometimes we operate out of fear: fear of something we may not want to hear or things we may see in ourselves that need to be changed or of the unknown. This fear is real to us as we go through change, experience change and try to resist change. Yet, this fear often stifles creativity and our ability to move to a deeper level.

As humans, we react in ways we've always reacted. We have tendencies to make things complex while weathering our storms. The lesson, though, should be to keep it simple. When I thought about what might help others, I wanted to keep it simple. I wanted to share experiences, provide insight about the ideas, and demonstrate practical applications to prompt others to think and move forward in their unique way. It boils down to identifying solutions in order to move forward…not just move, but move forward with increased awareness and in alignment with who you are…well that's simple enough. But people have to be ready to hear it and; unfortunately, at times, it often takes a significant event or seeds of discontent for that to occur.

Everyone's trigger to introspection of self will be different. As you read further, answer some of the questions or work through the exercises. Remember to look at who you are and what you do: discover yourself and discover a path that utilizes YOUR talents. You can have a life and career in alignment of *who* you are. And the work you do or the role you are in may change as you transform and continue your path in life. Each experience builds on every other one and prepares you for the future. What brought me here to write about change and how to navigate through it? Experiences. Experiencing change can be difficult but there's an approach to how to navigate it. As you weather your storm, keep yourself open to the ideas and processes introduced here.

SELF-REFLECTION MOMENT

Have events changed you?

Did you ask for these changes?

As you look at events in your life, how have you approached them? (i.e., experienced them and moved on without another thought? Rehashed the situation over and over?)

What are the lessons that past events are helping you to learn?

What are some of the feelings you have surrounding the change occurring in your life?

Have you asked people for feedback in how you approached change? What is their feedback? Is listening to that feedback a challenge?

CHAPTER 3

THE CLOUD OF AMBIGUITY: HOW DO YOU KNOW WHEN YOU'RE IN IT?

Kristi described a time where her smiles were depleted and she dragged from one day to the next without purpose. She couldn't explain this cycle she was in only that she felt in a slump. She was, in fact, in a Cloud of Ambiguity. The Cloud of Ambiguity occurs when the purpose and or vision is unclear, your thinking is fractious and you feel stressed or stuck. Purposeful action becomes particularly problematic during your Cloud of Ambiguity.

Kristi decided to seek out the one-on-one coaching program in The C Club®, that helps Cancer Conquerors reclaim, reshape and renew their life after cancer and navigate through their Cloud of Ambiguity.

She discovered that she navigates change through her natural motivators. She naturally creates order in all aspects of her work as an administrator, her life, and her relationships. Her approach worked for her until after her cancer treatment. After treatment, she felt like a different person but didn't know how to process her feelings and her life. Upon entering the coaching program, Kristi developed a vision that encapsulated her values. She also created a plan that was in alignment with her new vision. She took purposeful steps that moved her beyond her cloud. Day after day, she consciously focused on her vision for her future. She worked with her natural motivators of assembling order. She created an order from the scattered chaos she felt months earlier: An order she innately needed to move ahead. Most importantly, she learned how to approach things differently—not as she usually had. She used her innate motivator of creating order yet recognized when that motivator no longer worked and learned how to manage her other motivators.

She incorporated activities that aligned with her vision and her authentic self began to emerge. Her authentic self included not only the natural way she was motivated, but also her natural talents. Kristi's approach was often to collect information and data before she took action. She would take thought-out and calculated risks. When, and only when, she had these natural motivators or needs met, was she able to take action consistent with her vision. But she didn't realize that these same motivators, if left unmanaged, kept her stuck.

One of Kristi's natural talents was sewing pajama bottoms. The act of sewing is process work that also aligns with Kristi's natural motivators. She spoke of a plan to market the pajama bottoms. To her, it was a pastime that would feed her need for volunteer work. These were special pajamas. They were pajama bottoms that she sewed for children with cancer. Would she continue to make those pajama bottoms? Perhaps this was a momentary interest but an interest she would pursue at the moment. Perhaps it was a short-term idea that would be the catalyst to resolve another sticking point.

One day, Kristi talked about visiting the place where she had her chemotherapy to let the staff know about her new pajama bottom business venture. But she only talked about it—just talked and thought about it. When it came down to committing to a date to visit them, she wondered what held her back. She thought for a moment and remembered the smells of the chemotherapy office. She didn't want to revisit the office for that reason. She was afraid that the visit would trigger a physical reaction. Kristi was naturally motivated for creating safety, process, control, and order. Of course this motivation made her good at her work as an administrator organizing projects but now was her inhibitor. This visit also represented a risk to Kristi.

Is there fear? I asked. "Yes," she replied. "But of what?" She said aloud as if she was reasoning it out to herself. It was then that she set a date to visit the oncology unit. She had no real experience that she would encounter a physical reaction to the smells of the chemotherapy offices—only an assumption. She decided to test that assumption and take a risk outside of her natural motivator for cautiousness.

The day came for her to visit the oncology unit. She summoned the courage to follow through. After all, she made the commitment to herself to go. The staff appreciated seeing her and the visit gave them closure because most patients don't return to visit the health care staff. She commented that it felt to her a weight had been lifted off of her shoulders and it gave her closure.

She didn't get sick after all and she reconnected with the nurses. She summoned her bravery to move ahead on her commitment. She resolved her fear issue through her visitation to the chemotherapy office. She initially avoided this visit that she anticipated would be unharmonious but it cleared her mind moving her past her stuck point. The pajamas were a short-lived project yet a kind of creative internal healing consistent with how she was motivated and helped her make the visit to the oncology staff.

Much time has passed since Kristi visited the chemotherapy offices. Eventually, she left her corporate position and now enjoys a life filled with family and volunteer work—a life she designed, believed in, and took purposeful action to reshape after her life event.

Like Kristi, you know you're in your Cloud of Ambiguity when things are not clear, you are stressed, or taking purposeful action seems difficult. Does it seem that things are not quite working the way you have planned? Did an event or series of events have you stuck or questioning?

If so, you're in the Cloud of Ambiguity. Sometimes we try to work through it, avoid it, or try to see it. Sometimes we stay in it until we learn what we need to learn.

The Cloud of Ambiguity

This uncertainty, this ambiguity, can be unsettling particularly when we do not have a clear direction or solid foundation. Everyone's trigger into the Cloud of Ambiguity is different. If you went through a merger, job loss, divorce, business fluctuation, marriage, trauma, or illness, these are events that can catapult you into your Cloud of Ambiguity especially when your vision for the future was never solidified.

SELF-REFLECTION MOMENT

Is feeling afraid of or avoiding an event because of what you anticipate it will be an issue for you?

What if you addressed the situation?

Do you know when your natural urge for safety and control is emerging?

What are the possibilities if you worked outside of your safety zone or stretched it?

What needs to be resolved?

Do you know what motivates you?

Chapter Four

Where Am I?

Change can happen in an instant.
Transformation occurs over time.

When I meet people in career transition, I often hear "I don't know what to do or how to get there much less where to start." I often reply, "What do you know?" What makes up *who* you are? What are your talents? Working through your Cloud of Ambiguity is a discovery process.

As explained in Kristi's story, everyone has a set of innate motivators or authenticities inside that has helped them navigate through life. These motivators have us approach situations in certain ways and sometimes they produce results: results we intend, results we didn't intend, and, sometimes, these motivators get in our way.

We drive through life and are expected as a teenager to determine a path without first discovering *who* we are. We might have even been able to maneuver through our life yet not gain an understanding about our innate motivators, but they somehow got us through those life events.

If we first discover what truly motivates us, we might make different life choices, select better careers, find ways to reduce stress in our lives, and have better relationships.

When you are asked what do you want to do and you reply, "I don't know," ask yourself, "What do I know?" Instinctively what comes naturally for you? Do you relate well to people? Do you innately produce fact and figures? Do you naturally look for what's wrong with the picture or troubleshoot? Do you naturally develop processes? When you examine and develop your self-awareness and your relationships surrounding that awareness, you begin to work through your Cloud of Ambiguity.

Examining The Infinite Power Within.

Starting with yourself is the starting point when your path isn't quite clear.

What does it mean to examine your infinite power within? We have tendencies to look externally but, if you point at something, where are the other fingers on your hand pointing? Back at yourself? When you point at something else, you are avoiding looking at your self.

As I look back on my life as a child, I was bored in a traditional class and drifted off in thoughts of new ideas. I saw myself as smart in certain areas yet I felt defined by the low grades I received in mathematics early in childhood. Yet, I instinctively understood and easily connected with people.

In looking at the pivotal points in my life, one of the most powerful events was surviving cancer. Here I was in my late twenties and told "We found a malignancy." I stood at the foot of that massive mountain, looking up at the top, and feeling like a minute speck. I discovered that I was not immortal at twenty-something.

Over a decade later after conquering cancer, another kind of transition, career transition, would lead me to another path not yet taken. How could I possibly be in career transition? Although a strong performer, this transition was much bigger than I would have imagined. It would be the catalyst to greater things to come; yet, I would have to experience heartache and disappointment and sadness, and a range of emotions that, quite frankly, I just did not want to experience.

Through this transition, however, I learned many things about the tenacity that got me to this point. Hmmm, the same tenacity? Is this part of my infinite power within? Do I have a little something—resilience perhaps? Was there a greater purpose in store that I couldn't see at the moment? What are these innate navigational tools that I possess? Oddly enough, I learned that I helped others to see connections.

In discovering your infinite power within, how you approach your transitions can provide insights to your innate self (your motivators.) Many individuals feel a sense of loss when their jobs are eliminated, they retire, relationships end, or go through other transitions. They can't sleep, they become depressed, and the range of daily emotions feel like a roller coaster. Oftentimes in job loss they have deeply imbedded their jobs into *who* they are rather than imbedding who they are and doing what comes naturally. This embedding process takes place over time. How many times have you said, "Hello, this is [your name and title] from XYZ Company?" "Hello, I'm [your name], [Suzie's/John's] [spouse, child, mother, father, etc.]." You can embed yourself to a position, role or title and it is difficult to see yourself differently. But, at times, events occur and have us look at these roles. These events are opportunities to create something new.

Some people are naturally driven to forge ahead. However, if we forge ahead with the same intensity we always have, we won't see different results because we don't do or think of things differently. Or, if we forge ahead with the same process we have always used, we can continue to be stuck.

As you read ahead, remember that you can make a positive impact on your life. Your natural motivators and talents have gotten you where you are today. However, those same motivators become needs and can keep you stuck in a rut or prevent you from previewing possibilities. A rut that may have you saying:

- But I've done this job for twenty-five years and don't know anything else.

- I feel stuck after this illness.

- My whole life was _____, and now it's gone.

- I used to be a carefree person and I don't feel that anymore.

- I know I was good at what I do, but now I don't know anymore.

- I'm sick and tired of being sick and tired.

- Mandatory retirement—what do you mean I can't work here anymore?

- I don't like the way this event was handled.

This rut or, what feels like insurmountable stress and/ or frustration, (Cloud of Ambiguity), many times, unfortunately, comes after you experience a significant life event. But there is strength in discovering you.

We all have strengths and areas of improvement. Why is this important? It is part of aligning *who* you are and what you do, which may change over time as your self awareness deepens. We can change our behaviors but we will innately approach the way we do things by what motivates us. As we create more self-awareness about what innately fuels us, we can recognize when our motivators are not effective and how to work with them to get different results or examine alternatives.

Creating a deeper level of self awareness about how we approach life can be unnerving. Unnerving because we have to be responsible for the impact we have on our relationships and actions. We have to admit we aren't perfect and we have enhancement areas. These transitions can lead us to use our natural talents and/or motivators more deeply or regularly.

This self discovery can be a vastly different place especially when we work and play in cultures where our systems are built to tell everyone how great they are. To admit improvement or to want to enhance abilities is often a leadership quality, but all too often, it is not present in our work and relationship environments. The need to enhance our self awareness or to understand and maximize our talents is something we must acknowledge in order to move through our Cloud of Ambiguity.

SELF-REFLECTION MOMENT

Are you feeling like you are constantly climbing a mountain in your life?

Where are there disconnects?

Are there things you are forcing to happen right now?

What are your innate talents? (This is not asking how well you make widgets, but how do you approach making those widgets?)

Do you see what others don't?

Where are there connections in your life?

CHAPTER FIVE

DRIVING THROUGH THE CLOUD OF AMBIGUITY

Buckle your seatbelt and be prepared to take the ride of your life. Creating your self-awareness is often *the* starting point to answering the question: *Me, Myself, and Why?*

There are a number of ways we navigate through our Cloud of Ambiguity or change.

When you look at a map, do you look at where you want to go first before you identify where you are on the map? Believe it or not, some do, some don't depending on what motivates you. We know that the cloud looks different for everyone and each person is unique. When you create awareness about where you are before navigating, you can then come to terms with focus and action (or nonaction) that will be most meaningful and purposeful.

In your travels through this book, you will be introduced to characters and their natural motivations. Some situations may resonate with you stronger than others. When the words speak to you, underline them. After you read about each character, you may see your own motivators emerge. Once you create an awareness about what energizes you, you begin to take steps to change or manage that which aligns with your vision, motivators and future.

We have a tendency to navigate through our Cloud of Ambiguity with our natural motivators. Our natural motivators lead us to our safety zones—those areas where we naturally go—because of what motivates us and what we have learned. Our motivators take over, on auto pilot, and we operate without thought and without purposeful direction. Our motivators can be good and certainly allowed us to get through life. But when change occurs and this change is prompting transformation (or where we feel dissatisfied), then we may need to look at doing things differently to get different results.

As you look at the characters that follow, there are suggested solutions to prompt thought in how you can do things differently to get different results. Take the time to see how you identify with each of the characters' motivators. You may also want to identify the motivators of other people with whom you interact to help you resolve and improve your relationships.

HARMONIOUS HAZEL

Who is Harmonious Hazel?

Harmonious Hazel shies away from most conflict in her life and keeps a lot of that stress inside. Hazel didn't realize it but she works in fear: fear of not being good enough, knowing enough or hard working enough. She often says, I'm afraid or concerned that this or that will happen and spends a lot of time consumed in what others will think or say. She lives in "what if" trying to remove all barriers at times, before taking action. Hazel finds herself carefully weighing risks and sometimes takes no action because she has talked herself out of it or identifies all of the reasons why she shouldn't move on to the next step or take a risk.

Hazel enjoys a team environment and often gravitates toward participation on committees. She needs to be part of a team environment and seeks consensus from the team both in her interactions and decisions. She seeks this consensus especially if there are risky decisions. Her need for consensus and a team environment or approach are a part of Hazel's natural motivators as is her need to remove or retreat from conflict. These motivators can be her strengths because she works best with others. However, these motivators can also be inhibitors if she is unaware of them or they are left unmanaged especially when navigating change.

Hazel often thinks about leaving her job as an administrative assistant in a large company. Because of her perceived security of a steady paycheck, she remains in a position that is boring to her.

One day Hazel noticed a suspicious mole on her hand and had it checked by a doctor. She contacted the doctor the next day and found out what she didn't want to hear...that it was malignant. This event placed Hazel in her Cloud of Ambiguity because she didn't have a team, she was in unfamiliar territory (risk to her) and didn't know what would happen.

When Harmonious Hazel found out about her malignancy, she didn't want anyone to know about her condition.

She discovered a team of doctors that walked her through the treatment process. This team of doctors on several levels met her innate motivators: a team approach that helped minimize her perceived risk in moving through unknown territory.

Hazel went through treatment. After three months and a clean bill of health, the doctor told her to come back in another three months. Three months? That would be an eternity! What happened to every month? What if it comes back (wanting to avoid the risk)? What happened to my team of doctors (needs a team)! I feel thrust in to ambiguity…again!

She was never a cancer conqueror and is stifled to be on her own after this event. This is a new event to her. This event changed Hazel. Different areas in her life became important to her. That job she despised? She now thinks about taking action to change it. She doesn't know how to change her current situation, but knows she feels unhappy. Life seems different to her now.

What impact does the cancer experience have on Hazel's life? Hazel feels isolated and disengaged. She is stuck in her Cloud of Ambiguity and has become unusually quiet and introspective. She feels like she has no handle on her life and where it is headed.

Emerging Hazel

Historically, Hazel sought harmony. She didn't realize she interrupted her idea making. She dismissed her ideas because of perceived obstacles—that natural need to seek harmony and avoid risk. She disliked debate about ideas because she saw it as conflict but never recognized that in herself. She was not self-aware of who she innately was—that auto pilot—those natural or innate motivators that she needed to get met. Hazel views all sides of an issue by gathering other people's opinions, which is why she liked the team of doctors. She didn't realize that she needs to get other people's viewpoints before decision making especially with new experiences. After her bout with cancer, she remains in her safety zone but her experience with illness gave her pause to look inside herself...at her real self.

While she works well in a team and that natural motivator can be a strength, in times of change, this motivator needs to be managed. In order to get unstuck, Hazel may need to embrace other behaviors or tools to help her move beyond her Cloud of Ambiguity. She may need to ask herself, how *can* it be done (whatever "it" is). Remember that Hazel naturally gravitates toward minimizing risk. In the effort to minimize risk, she spends a great deal of time preparing for things and thinking about every potential barrier.

It is not always possible to remove all risk. When a person like Hazel wants to naturally remove conflict or what she perceives as a barrier, she needs to focus on the problem. She may also need to look at what is or isn't risk. Debating ideas or views, to Hazel, comes across to her as conflict. Therefore to Hazel, there is a risk in conflict and that is naturally draining for her. She may avoid or delay an action, a person or a conversation or not make a decision because of her natural need to remove that conflict.

Hazel's natural motivator is also being part of a team. The team allows Hazel to think through and validate ideas. She seeks out a situation where she is part of a team. This is a strength but in times of transition can inhibit her from moving ahead when independent decisions need to be made.

As Hazel moves through her Cloud of Ambiguity and begins to confront the issues, it's important for her to create an awareness about who she innately is and when her natural motivators take over. She needs to realize her apprehension to risk and conflict are natural for her. She will need to acknowledge that not all barriers can be removed, not all debate is conflict, and she may have to work independent of a team.

Her acceptance that just because someone has an opinion different than hers or because someone reacts or doesn't agree with something Hazel does or says, doesn't make Hazel or her idea wrong or the other right—just different.

Harmonious Hazel's Solutions to Navigate Forward

If you identify with Harmonious Hazel and experience transition, become aware of when your motivation for belonging to the team or your tendency to retreat from difficult situations emerges. If you are disconnected from that team environment, you also may have difficulty letting go of what you had and thinking of or entertaining new possibilities for your life. Consider the following:

- Notice when you retreat or hesitate from participating in an event or situation. Ask yourself, what one step can I take to address the situation? What positive step can I take next time?

- If in transition, join a related networking team, a support group or club to get that need for interaction met, especially if you spend a significant amount of time alone. There is a balance between getting the need met and managing it.

- Volunteer and become active in group activities.

- Hire a coach to help you work through the transition.

- Give yourself a time limitation to think through the next steps or identify timelines for yourself and stick to those timelines.

- Get feedback from others on how well you are communicating (i.e., is the focus on the negative (barriers) or the positive (possibilities)). Be open to the feedback.

- Recognize that you may gravitate toward what you know, because it is safe and less risky.

Interacting with Hazel

If you interact with Harmonious Hazel, understand that she has an innate ability to be a team player but may be perceived as not saying what is on her mind especially if she believes she is in a conflict or debating situation. Hazel naturally seeks harmony. She does not intend to avoid conflict, however, she may not feel safe enough in the situation to share her ideas. Debating ideas can be an energy bleed for her. When you interact with Hazel:

- Acknowledge her contributions and consider her ideas.

- When Hazel gets stuck, ask her what might limit her ability to interact with the team or to make a decision. (Remember your tone when asking this question. If Hazel feels she is in conflict, she may retreat further.)

- Ask her how you can help her in the decision-making process.

- Actively listen to what she has to say without debate or comment—which she may see as conflict.

- What can you do differently so that Hazel fully expresses herself during conversation and interaction?

SELF-REFLECTION MOMENT FOR HARMONIOUS HAZEL

How does not participating in a conversation where there is debate or conflict impact you and others? Does it cause you stress?

If you vacillate on a decision, ask yourself what does waiting for a decision do and/or not do for you? What is holding you back?

Is fear or concern about rejection of yourself or of your ideas an issue?

Do you operate out of the assumption that you don't want to bother others with your thoughts and feelings? What is that doing for you?

Is concern with what others might think of you inhibiting possibilities or results from being realized?

Are you concerned with making the perfect choice?

Are your concerns preventing you from exploring your full potential?

Are you delaying a decision that, in the big picture, is not what's most important? What is most important?

Are there decisions you can make in spite of things you are avoiding?

What is possible if you could be the authentic you?

AUDACIOUS ADAM

Who is Audacious Adam?

Adam gets excited when he thinks of new projects, ideas, and ways to make money. He is an independent-minded person who needs a lot of freedom to express himself, his ideas and his work. Adam wants to do what Adam wants to do. He has always navigated through life this way.

Adam likes to make swift decisions. He thrives in a competitive environment. This competitiveness allows him to be successful in his job—(winning IT contracts, managing projects, etc.—a strength.) However, Adam's focus on new things and ideas can be an inhibitor for him. He doesn't stop long enough to complete one idea before going on to the next. This swiftness often creates chaos in his work environment. He attacks any new situation much like he probably has attacked other projects, relationships, and work: makes assumptions, quick assessments or judgments. While this approach may have worked for him in some cases, other people perceive Adam as arrogant. He often enters situations with an assumption that he is the expert even without the required skills or knowledge. While his natural motivators (to think of new things, act on *his* ideas, and to work independently) can be strengths, especially when he creates new concepts, ideas, or business ventures, these motivators, if left unmanaged, can also be weaknesses when navigating change or working with others.

With his competitiveness, Adam is also energized when he debates concepts, ideas and other conversations. This debate style is seen as conflict by Harmonious Hazel. Because she looks at debating as arguing or conflict, Hazel may have had a really good idea, but holds back that idea. Adam doesn't realize the impact that his desire to debate or his natural need to talk over others has on the other person.

When his job as Vice President of Information Technology was eliminated, he became outwardly angry. He confronted the decision with his former employer and threatened to take them to court. He thought he could win. Winning is important to Adam.

Adam thought that the decision to downsize his position could be conquered and that it was just wrong. In fact, Adam believes he can conquer anything—whatever "it" is—and this situation was no different.

While he decided whether or not to pursue a lawsuit with his former employer, Adam thought about the people-oriented company culture he worked in. He knew that he was different than his counterparts and, at times, tried to be less competitive and relate to people. He tried to connect with the team and take action on the team's ideas—not his own. He realized this team environment took a lot of energy from him. Adam was competitive and needed his independence yet worked in a culture where there were many teams and consensus was the norm. Many times, Adam didn't get to implement Adam's projects, improvements, and thought processes.

One day prior to his job's downsizing, out of sheer exhaustion, he said, "I don't know if I can continue to do this job, I don't know if I can change." Did he need to change *who* he was innately or should he spend his energy creating an environment where he could be *who* he was—and who he was with a level of self-awareness and management of those motivators? Did he need to change his approach slightly to get different results? Was his job loss a gift after all?

Emerging Adam

People choose careers according to what their interests are at the time without developing any self-awareness of what really motivates them. Twenty years later, these same individuals discover that they hate the job they did, but they get so used to the lifestyle they don't know how to change or to do anything differently. When a job loss or illness strikes, it is only then that people take stock in what kind of life they want to lead.

Historically, Audacious Adam dismissed others' ideas or adopted them and made those ideas his own without giving credit to the contributors. People have shared that his comments are perceived as short or edgy and he is only concerned about the financial results, the task at hand and doesn't work well on teams.

Adam got frustrated and angry when he couldn't immediately change his employer's mind about eliminating his position. Adam's anger arose because he didn't feel in control or that it was his idea to leave the company. Like many people who have experienced job loss, there is a period where they feel like the air has just been let out of their balloon.

If Adam doesn't let go of the anger he feels toward his employer, he might continue with interview after interview and wonder why he didn't get the job. Of course, if Adam doesn't become self aware of his natural need for independence and the impact his natural need to discuss *his* ideas or debate issues has on others, he might always think it is the other person's fault when things don't work. He needs to discover how he could approach people differently to make sure he is listening to other people's ideas in an open and direct, but not confronting, manner. He may also not be aware that his desire to win or debate can prevent real results from happening.

Adam charged through life with assumptions. Without testing those assumptions, he has gotten himself stuck, yet charged forward with those assumptions especially when it came to relationships. If he saw that relationships weren't benefiting him, he would drop those relationships because they weren't useful at the time—never revisiting them or providing a second chance.

This is the time where Adam can learn how to create a balanced environment of idea sharing, open up to different opportunities where he has the independence to make decisions, and discover how to best utilize his natural motivators in a way that is even more effective.

If you identify with Audacious Adam, ask yourself:

- What is success to you?

- Is there something getting in the way of real success?

- If you identify with Audacious Adam, is there something you want but are preventing yourself from having by advocating your way?

- What do your relationships look like? How do you know?

- What assumptions do you find yourself making as it relates to relationships, career, business, family, etc.?

In order for Adam to move beyond his Cloud of Ambiguity, he will need to create an understanding about his motivators and manage them when they alienate others or get in his way of things that are necessary and important.

Once Adam begins to manage his natural motivators, he steps outside of his unrestrained audacity. He realizes he can get things done but that the foundation of a strong leader is self-awareness and managing those natural motivators, those needs. Adam learns to ask for feedback so that he understands the impact he has on others. He embraces his independent-mindedness and allows others to also have their independence and decision making. While he realizes he micromanages or overturns other people's decisions, he creates a tolerance to let others learn from their mistakes. He creates an environment where there is idea sharing and acknowledgement. While he naturally believes he has strong ownership over decisions, he resists the urge to override other people's decisions. Adam learns to monitor how and what he communicates to others. The key is in the balance between listening to ideas from others and creating Adam's agenda.

Audacious Adam's Solutions to Navigate Forward

If you identify with Audacious Adam, solutions to navigate through change may include:

- Implement listening techniques. You may need to take a different approach to get different results.

Give the critical inner voice (that gives you negative thoughts of yourself and others) something
else to do during a conversation through listening
tools.

- Practice allowing others to act on their ideas—not
your ideas. If their idea does not work out and you
want to criticize it, try instead, asking the other
person what they could have been done differently
rather than immediately giving your insight.

- Allow yourself down time. Audacious Adam has
no trouble thinking of new ideas. However, Adam
needs to learn to be still enough to see the path
he's on. Oftentimes, if you are like Audacious
Adam, you push ahead and may miss messages
because you spend too much of your time and
energy undertaking new concepts as well as trying to make each concept work without having a
thought out plan. Going nowhere fast?

- Avoid the urge to quickly dismiss people who
you think may not be relevant to your thinking
or helpful to you in any way. Be open to the pos-
sibility that there may be a time where a relationship with that person may enrich your life or that
you may be instrumental in their life. Remember,
Audacious Adam can come across with what is
described as short or curt when communicating.
If you relate to him, how do others perceive your
line of questioning—ask them! Absorb the feedback they give you—don't debate it.

- If you can identify with Audacious Adam <u>and</u> you are in an environment where you act on *other* people's ideas, you may be unmotivated because you are unable to act on your ideas. If you are in this environment, you may need to look at other areas where you can think of ideas, concepts and things and are able to execute your ideas. In this case, you may want to involve yourself in other areas to generate those ideas, concepts or things— even if it is away from your work environment. Creating and taking action on your ideas can be a strength and a weakness. Raise your level of awareness when it is not working for you.

Interacting with Audacious Adam

If you interact with a person like Audacious Adam, understand that they like a challenge and winning their way is important. They need to feel like they've put their authorization on a concept or idea.

Understand that they appreciate a challenge and debating the idea is comfortable for them. While debating may be demotivating for you, it is comfortable for Adam, and he expects it, may foster it, and needs it. Make sure your conversations are results-oriented and factual in nature.

SELF-REFLECTION MOMENT FOR AUDACIOUS ADAM

If you identify with Adam, what approaches or ideas do *you* have that will fundamentally change the way you have done things, approached your transition or interacted in your relationships?

If you really want do something different to get different results, communicate to others that you are committed to acknowledge other people's ideas, concepts, and processes. Ask them to provide you with feedback when you are and aren't demonstrating awareness to the change and react positively to the feedback by thanking them when you do receive it.

Ask yourself:

- Do you want to win? If so, why is that important?

- Are you talking about only your ideas or agenda?

- Is acknowledging other people's ideas difficult for you? How do you know?

- Are winning arguments or your way important?

- What does arguing, winning, and/or debating give you? Is there a balance?

- What does it take away from you?

- What's missing?

- What is the best environment for you?

- What can acceptance of others, of self, bring?

ANALYTICAL ANN

Who is Analytical Ann?

Analytical Ann is naturally an introspective and logical thinker. When you shake Ann's hand, you'll see her unassuming and factual style emerge. Ann works in the telecommunications area and her division is merging with another division. As a result of this merger, she experiences many last-minute changes.

At times, when under pressure or when tasking (that is, involved in a project with steps and needs to complete them), others will notice her brusque response when they interrupt her. While the interrupter views their disruption as important, Analytical Ann looks at the interruption as unproductive relative to the task at hand.

Her concern is to get tasks done and social chit-chat or digressions are often difficult for her. However, she has enjoyed the part of her job where she is left alone to communicate through emails because this gives her time to think about what she wants to say and time to think through decisions. She also likes to check tasks off her list and handle them herself rather than delegating to her team.

When she develops a structure, has been notified of changes and is allowed uninterrupted time to think through projects or decisions, she is energized. These are Ann's motivators, something she needs and can be Ann's strengths, if managed.

Yet, the merger has placed Ann in her Cloud of Ambiguity. She receives last-minute changes, many interruptions and, thus, doesn't know what work priority to place first and how to best communicate them.

Ann needs to realize that she may have to manage her needs or natural motivators. She may have to verbalize her thoughts in order to let others know she needs to be left alone to complete her tasks. When Analytical Ann verbalizes what she thinks (versus keeping it inside), she can improve trust among her team. This technique may help Analytical Ann navigate through the merger (her Cloud of Ambiguity).

Emerging Analytical Ann

Recently, Ann attended a social event and spent small amounts of time in group discussion but removed herself from the group where she could be alone. While some people perceived this as unsocial, Ann inherently needed this time alone because it was draining for her to be with a group of new people from the other division.

How do Ann's natural motivators affect her during the merger selection process? By the sheer nature of the interviewing process (question and on-the-spot answering), Ann doesn't have an opportunity to think about the questions. She may often undersell her talents if the interviewer isn't aware that Ann needs time to answer the questions. It is important for someone who identifies with Analytical Ann to prepare for interviews. The time leading up to the interview can be stressful for Ann but can be reduced by reviewing potential interview questions, updating a resume, and practicing her answers.

In relationships, Analytical Ann does not verbalize her discontent—leaving others with guesswork which often creates confusion and more uncertainty until the day when she has had enough and you see an uncharacteristic eruption. Because she thinks internally instead of out loud, this internal process can be perceived by others as suspicious. People often wonder what's on Ann's mind. However, when she has completed her think time, the output is usually work or process of great quality: a significant strength.

Analytical Ann's Solutions to Navigate Forward

If you relate to Analytical Ann, remember to:

- Practice verbalizing what you are thinking using caution with how the message is being delivered. Often others won't know your plan at resolving an issue if you don't verbalize it.

- Accept help. Ann believes that she needs to figure it out herself. While that may be noble, it may not always be in everyone's best interest, including hers.

- Let people know you need time to think about it and give them and yourself a deadline. This will help to communicate that you need the alone time to resolve your issue.

- Bring awareness that when you're tasking, your answers may be brusque in delivery. You may need to verbalize what you need (limited interruptions, etc.) in order to be most effective.

- Make a decision and develop a plan—but give yourself a timeline for getting your plan completed. Resist the natural urge to lament or over plan your project.

- Get feedback from others on your effectiveness in communication with others.

- Record your thoughts of your achievements in a journal. This helps you to remember your accomplishments so that you can share them at performance review time or during an interview.

Interacting with Analytical Ann

If you interact with someone like Analytical Ann, give her time to think about things, particularly if it is a new idea, thought or process. If Ann has already developed an expertise in that area, she will provide a well-thought out immediate response, however. Don't always assume Ann needs to think about it. Also, limit the number of interruptions.

After a meeting, give time for people like Ann to process their thoughts because her best ideas come about an hour after that meeting. Once her need to think ideas through is met, you will receive thought-out ideas.

SELF-REFLECTION MOMENT FOR ANALYTICAL ANN

What one step can you take to communicate differently?

The next time you need to respond, how can you phrase it constructively?

Why is it important to convey your thoughts, feelings, and ideas in groups?

What happens when you don't convey your thoughts, feelings and ideas?

SPIRITED SANDY

Who is Spirited Sandy?

Spirited Sandy is an extrovert who likes encouragement and appreciation for her work. She has an innate need to give and get help from others and is naturally empathetic. Unlike Analytical Ann, Sandy likes to talk out loud to generate ideas and concepts and has the natural ability to connect with others. She has a long and successful career in selling and while she may be unaware of it, she seeks acknowledgement of her ideas from others. In fact, if she feels constantly rejected or her ideas are not acknowledged, she stops sharing her thoughts altogether. She often feels energized when she interacts or participates in activities with people; in fact, she seeks them out through networking or visiting with others in the office.

Spirited Sandy is in career transition and was recently laid off from her position as Sales Representative. She is home alone and feels generally hopeless in her search. Her energy level is really low. The lay off placed Sandy in her Cloud of Ambiguity where she doesn't know which way to turn or the next step to take.

Sandy's challenge is to find the balance between getting her motivators met and managing them. Spirited Sandy innately needs people interaction but does not get that innate motivator met on a daily basis (she is home alone). She often needs to talk through issues to resolve them. If she is unable to talk through her career transition to help her resolve it, she may get stuck further because she has no outlet. This could drastically impair her ability to move through her Cloud of Ambiguity. She feels disconnected and doesn't know how to reconnect.

One day, Spirited Sandy gravitated toward her natural ability to connect with people by joining a career networking group. She is naturally articulate and did most of the talking rather than managing her need to communicate. She needed to be fully present when others conveyed their ideas yet she interrupted others to get her ideas through, which didn't help her cause. She went into overdrive trying to get her motivators met.

While Spirited Sandy also naturally wants to help others, this need to help often places her in problem-solving mode. Sometimes, the other person just wants Sandy to listen yet Sandy wants to solve the problem or develop ideas. This innate motivator is natural for Sandy and she feels she is being helpful. However, it depends what the other person wants, needs and is ready for—which is not always someone giving her thoughts and ideas to solve a problem.

Emerging Spirited Sandy

Spirited Sandy does not realize that she talks about herself, her issues and ideas or repeats herself often. She does this because her natural tendency is to verbally resolve issues. She also needs to be careful not to rehash negative issues over and over again as she has a strong need to be heard and acknowledged.

If Sandy were to look at her motivators, she would realize that she is naturally persuasive; however, she needs to recognize that the art of listening can be more powerful than the art of persuasion. She is aware that the more the other person talks, the more *she* can learn and, often, more meaningful conversations occur and deepen. Active listening is often a learning opportunity for other people who identify with Spirited Sandy. If Spirited Sandy really wants a job, her natural tendency will be to sell herself or ideas rather than to listen to what the interviewer says. While her natural motivator to persuade can work for her, it can also be a detriment if left unrestrained.

Spirited Sandy's Solutions to Navigate Forward

- Listen to others and resist the innate need for your own acknowledgement of your ideas;

- Join networking groups and practice your listening skills;

- Allow yourself to talk through issues but seek a balance.

- Allow yourself to be in the moment and to not react to a situation.

Interacting with Spirited Sandy

If you interact with Spirited Sandy, encourage her with positive reinforcement (i.e., you can do it, what a great person you are for thinking about that solution, what you are saying is…, etc.) Spirited Sandy responds well to positive reinforcement. In fact, Sandy needs to know she has been heard by responding with a verbal "I understand," head nod or other verbal response.

If you listen to a person like Spirited Sandy, ask that person to develop a timeline when they will move to solution building. When Spirited Sandy gets stuck, she naturally wants to talk about how stuck she is; however, that can leave her fixated on the negative. Sandy needs to do something different by focusing on the positive and on what she can control.

SELF-REFLECTION MOMENT FOR SPIRITED SANDY

If you relate to Spirited Sandy, what's important when someone's talking?

Is acceptance and/or acknowledgement important to you?

Is accommodating others an issue?

What one step can you take to change your current situation?

JUGGLER JANE

Who is Juggler Jane?

Juggler Jane is the President of a small service company that has seen some hard times. She has been accustomed to juggling multiple tasks and is seen as a driving personality that gets things done. She often gets impatient standing in lines and you will see her tapping her fingers and showing her impatience verbally or through behavioral cues (tapping foot, looking at her watch, etc.)

Jane also procrastinates on things that are routine or repetitive (like bookkeeping, typing long projects or filing.) This creates added pressure and stress on Jane. She has a short attention span, especially with people who are more methodical. She interrupts others with another question when they haven't finished answering her first question.

Emerging Juggler Jane

Juggler Jane doesn't realize that she places pressure on others by requesting that tasks be completed urgently. She interrupts when people talk and, depending on the pressure, may cut people off altogether when they are talking. Because she has the innate ability to process information quickly, she waves her hand (as if to hurry someone up) if she does not get the information quickly enough. Her staff often feels the pressure in her urgency. Traditional school settings and meetings are difficult for her to sit through. If Juggler Jane doesn't know where she is going, how fast do you think Juggler Jane tries to get there? Fast.

Before she can manage motivators, Juggler Jane needs to realize that she places pressure on herself and others.

She may even procrastinate to create that pressure that she works so well under; however, she expects others to work on her timeframe. She has a difficult time determining the amount of time it takes to get things done and shortchanges those timelines. These unrealistic timeframes put pressure on herself and, thus, on others who work for Jane.

Jane has always operated this way and realizes something needs to change. Her employee satisfaction survey results brought awareness that her sense of urgency can have a negative impact on her employees.

On the survey results, Juggler Jane is viewed as intense and reactive to change. Consequently, being in the moment is so difficult for Jane because of her impatience. If you relate to Juggler Jane, you may need to temper the need for haste with patience and tolerance of other people and consider their schedules.

Juggler Jane can use her transition time to refocus, reclaim, and rejuvenate her life as a whole. She spins her wheels and needs to do something different: to be in the moment.

Juggler Jane's Solutions to Navigate Forward

- Utilize listening techniques and allow enough time for people to complete their thoughts.

- Help yourself to be in the moment by focusing on what the other person says and layer the conversation. That is, take a portion of what the other person has said and use it in your next question to them.

- When your impatience for getting things done places undo pressure on others, this produces stress on everyone. Create an awareness on the way your behaviors impact others and carefully consider timelines when setting dates.

Interacting with Juggler Jane

If you interact with Juggler Jane, it will be important to set realistic timeframes. She will have the tendency to think things don't take as long as they actually do. While she likes her information quickly and expects others to respond to pressure as she does, Jane may not realize the pressure she places on others. She wants to hurry through processes and conversations, often shortcutting decisions. Because of her high urgency level, it is necessary to help Juggler Jane set realistic goals and avoid over commitment.

SELF-REFLECTION MOMENT FOR JUGGLER JANE

- Are you unfocused and juggling multiple things?

- Is everything urgent?

- What's most important?

- What advantages might you gain by waiting?

- Is responding to every request necessary?

- What would be possible if you set timeframes farther ahead than you naturally want to?

- Is your schedule managing you?

CALM CHRIS

Who is Calm Chris?

While Juggler Jane likes and needs to juggle a variety of projects and proceeds with a sense of urgency, Calm Chris deals with issues, projects and ideas with the underlying process in mind. This is a natural strength of Calm Chris.

Chris is a financial advisor whom others often view as an easy-going person. He naturally makes checklists and gives his full attention to one thing at a time yet. Calm Chris is a member of multiple clubs and enjoys the camaraderie of those associations. He has thought for quite some time about starting his business. Chris is stifled in his work environment because his company has gone through multiple mergers. He feels the pressure of unrealistic timeframes and doesn't feel that the new culture aligns with his natural talent for maintaining relationships and designing thoughtful processes.

It has taken many seeds of discontentment for Calm Chris to move on to new employment. Not a spur-of-the-moment decision for him, he made sure his exit strategy from his company was carefully planned out.

Chris' natural motivation is to create a plan or process. On one recent vacation, he created an in-depth itinerary. There were names, contact numbers, and timeframes. He plotted through that list carefully and with great precision creating a process that he innately needed.

Emerging Calm Chris

Calm Chris doesn't like pressure. When he is in the

Cloud of Ambiguity (prior to making the decision to leave) he found it difficult to take action or make decisions. He doesn't realize that, at times, others perceive him as plodding along and not responding to change. Yet the environment he worked in was not congruent with the natural way he navigated through his work. He eventually created the strategy that would help him move ahead.

Calm Chris naturally affiliates with others and is conscious of his need to create order in his environment. He tapped into his affiliates before starting his own company (part of his exit strategy). As owner of his new company, he is allowed to respond to his own time tables and created processes of great efficiencies. He found that when he works in an environment that allows him to use his natural motivators, he is energized and feels accomplished. Just as important, his clients appreciate the process that he put them through to understand their finances.

Calm Chris' Solutions to Navigate Forward

- Create a checklist for yourself and follow through and understand when you may have to circumvent some steps to move ahead.

- If you are told of a change that places you in your Cloud, keep in mind what you do well: you have strong relationships with people you know and can develop plans that are organized and thorough.

- Look for opportunities that allow your natural talents to emerge in an environment where you are appreciated for creating order, systems and processes.

- Be aware that you may resist change when it is sudden and unplanned.

Interacting with Calm Chris

If you interact with Calm Chris, remember that long-term affiliations are important. Before getting right into the business of the day, ask how he is and listen to the answer. Chris will appreciate that approach.

Chris's natural strength is to also create a process or order. This is a strength as long as you give Chris the space to do what he does best: create a thorough organized process, develop an order and form long-term relationships.

SELF-REFLECTION MOMENT FOR CALM CHRIS

- What's most important for your life?

- Can someone else help in getting things done?

- What can you delegate to accomplish your plan?

- What environment will feed well into your affiliation strength—that ability to formulate long-term relationships?

- Where is there stress in your life?

- What is contributing to the stress?

- In which environments are you using your natural strengths?

FLEXIBLE FRAN

Who is Flexible Fran?

Flexible Fran is an independent sales manager and has been in a position where she is required to follow through on many details often performing routine administrative work herself. She naturally wants to delegate those details, but, because of her work environment she cannot delegate these specifics.

She has the natural ability to develop out-of-the-box ideas and likes to operate in the gray area. She is casual in her communication style. Fran has been de-energized in her current role for some time. She arrives home after a full day of checking on the routine details of her work and doesn't have enough energy for her family.

She finds it hard to follow through on a lot of her detailed work and she received an average performance evaluation. She entered her Cloud of Ambiguity because she doesn't quite know how to change her environment.

Emerging Flexible Fran

Flexible Fran doesn't realize that she promises things to others without checking into the parameters or infrastructure of the organization. She often tells her clients that her company will be able to service the account but hasn't checked on the details to see if what she promised could be delivered. This gray area has created chaos in her business environment, especially with the Accounting and Information Technology Departments.

She naturally doesn't need a lot of information to make a decision which is reflected in how others have had to follow through on issues after her. Flexible Fran views structures and processes as hindrances or necessary evils to accomplish the task at hand. She completes most tasks but this level of detail has de-energized her and developed mistrust with her coworkers who are concerned they will have to pick up the slack.

One day, when negotiating a contract, Flexible Fran realized the hard way that she doesn't need a lot of information to make a decision and the details should be left to her team. She not only made an assumption about what the company needed, she missed a comma in a contract costing the company millions of dollars. While she builds a team that follows through for her on missing information or details, she alone was responsible for this contract. In this case, she should have maximized their strengths and included them on reviewing the contract language to make sure she had thoroughly executed her plan. She understands that the strengths of others who think plans through are helpful to her—not a hindrance.

Flexible Fran's Solutions to Navigate Forward

Flexible Fran realized she doesn't always follow through to the level of detail others expect. She realized that she naturally resists making lists, yet, this lack of follow through may be the issue that keeps her revisiting similar lessons and situations. Fran learns to maximize electronic systems that remind her of things to follow up on, especially if Flexible Fran doesn't have administrative support.

This latest contract issue illuminated her lack of follow through and the team doesn't trust her. They view her as unreliable because she makes promises but forgets to meet her commitments to the degree of detail they may expect.

Because Fran often finds it difficult to follow through on tasks and commitments she makes to others, the same issues recur and it has led to team trust issues. This can be a powerful learning opportunity if Fran chooses to create awareness about when her natural motivators to think outside of the box create unusual ideas and when this same talent inhibits her from successful outcomes.

If you identify with Flexible Fran, other solutions include:

- Understand that you may create ideas but remember to follow through or find a way to meet your commitments. Use a recorder or calendar to jot down promises or commitments you made.

- Identify clear expectations on next steps to make sure the parties are in agreement.

- Know your audience when communicating your thoughts and ideas. Resist the natural urge to say it like you see it. Recognize when your casual approach is working or not working for you.

If you're like Fran and are stuck in work of a routine or detailed nature and are no longer feeling challenged, think of solutions that would relieve you of routine work. Understand that others may not share your view that rules are meant to be bent and that they can bring that strength of structure and thoroughness into a situation.

Interacting with Flexible Fran

Are you interacting with someone like Flexible Fran where there are things falling through the cracks? It may be necessary to have Fran identify dates when there will be follow up, and the level of follow through. She also may need someone to help her follow through with the details. Someone wired more like Conscientious Connie (the next character) or Calm Chris may be a good complement.

SELF-REFLECTION MOMENT FOR FLEXIBLE FRAN

- What one thing can you do differently to improve some of the follow through issues or attend to details in your situation or commitments?

- What can you do to give others the requisite details and information they need to do their job?

- Where do you act on ideas without thinking them through?

- What is a source of frustration for you? How can you look at your situation, work, or environment differently given what you know about how Flexible Fran operates?

CONSCIENTIOUS CONNIE

Who is Conscientious Connie?

While Flexible Fran is often undaunted by feedback received, Conscientious Connie likes and needs information, structure and constructive feedback. Connie has a need to get everything perfect. In fact, she worries a great deal about the exactness of her work. She does not make a decision until she gets all of the information and, at times, this information collection impedes her progress. She has not found a balance between her need for information and exactness and the ability to move ahead and take a calculated but educated guess and risk.

Conscientious Connie likes to avoid criticism to such a degree it is often the other person's issue or fault. This can be a detriment as Conscientious Connie tries to navigate through change. She often puts up road blocks or thinks of ways things won't work. She delays decision making and this delay results in lost opportunities. This delay in decision making can be frustrating for those who interact with Connie.

Recently, Conscientious Connie took on responsibilities as a supervisor. Her critical eye allows her to see the details of her own and others' work and one of the reasons she was asked to take on responsibilities to review policies and procedures. Conscientious Connie has an innate need for information before she makes a decision. She often sees the pitfalls of a solution and strives for perfection. This can be a strength and a weakness. Because she puts her heart and soul into whatever she does, getting feedback from others that may identify a different or better way, can be difficult for Connie. When it comes to decision making, if information is lacking or if Connie doesn't have all of the answers, Conscientious Connie doesn't make a decision or delays it.

Connie has an interesting background. She is innately a creative being and spent many years in art school. While there, she met an instructor who was more like an unrestrained Audacious Adam. While Connie knew that her paintings were raw in technique, she took the instructor's criticism to heart. One day, the instructor delivered criticism that struck Connie to her core. The feedback completely set her back. It is not so much what the feedback was, but what she allowed it to do. She took that criticism so much to heart, she began pursuing another career path. She eventually began work for an organization that utilized some of her drawing talents and, later to a supervisory position. Painting would always take a back seat. Her work was safe and steady and provided a stable income for her family—something she didn't believe she would have been afforded as an artist. Remember, the thoroughness that drove her –what made her great at painting (her attention to detail) - also made her take the criticism to heart years earlier. She often plays life safe.

Would awareness about her innate motivators and artistry talent have been able to keep her grounded on what was important to her? Were there other things more important to her at the time?

How often do we take the safe and steady path rather than forge ahead with our innate talents? While reading this example some people might say: but working in an organization provided for her family. Indeed, it provided for the family; however, it may not have had to be an "either or" or "this or that." It could have included an "AND." This AND that. Working for an organization providing a regular income, AND working on the paintings. She could have utilized her innate motivators AND work that utilizes her innate talents. Connie may not see that option if she looks at doing things only one way, choosing "this OR that." Connie often lived in extremes. She looked at why things won't work versus how things can work. Interestingly, this was an innate talent—to spot what won't work or could be better.

Connie often said that she let go of that creative artist. Later on, she paused to think for a moment. She wondered if she was really at peace with letting go of that talent. Did she still seek out that innate talent that lay within? Did she pursue the path she was destined to pursue or did she work within her safety zone and without awareness? Connie would resurrect her painting talent.

Emerging Conscientious Connie

Connie acknowledges that she has a strong talent to identify what does not work. However she may have to work outside of her inherent need to look at the barriers in order to move ahead. Connie needs to determine what is most important as she moves ahead in her career. She often obsesses over a decision, when, in the full picture, the level of detail she strives for can impede her progress.

Her strength is in her attention to detail. Not everyone has that natural talent. She recognizes that her need to seek to understand may be perceived as not a big picture thinker because she may be asking questions about the details. It does not mean she is not a big picture thinker. However, she may lose others who do not share that high attention to detail. A Conscientious Connie needs to acknowledge and assume responsibility for errors but needs to feel safe in her environment without fear of retribution or punishment in order for her to maximize her natural motivator.

As Connie emerges her self-awareness, she understands that she critiques or judges an opportunity before she has experienced it. If you're like Conscientious Connie, you may find new experiences stressful. However, once you have experienced them, you become more comfortable with it and, naturally become an expert in them. Connie also has a tendency to remove all barriers before a decision is made. Connie seeks information to make that decision and, in transition times, it is often difficult to have all of the information before moving forward. The challenge for Connie is to work in unfamiliar areas more comfortably.

Conscientious Connie's Solutions to Navigate Forward

- Avoid analysis paralysis. If you identify with Connie, you may over analyze a situation—the right clothes to pack for vacation, just the right wording on a cover letter—to avoid any risk. During the Cloud of Ambiguity, come to terms that there is no such thing as perfection.

- Let go of what was and explore what can be without parameters, without judgments, and without thoughts of can't or shouldn't.

- Feedback is just feedback. It doesn't mean you did a horrible job or that you're not a good person; rather, it is something to learn from. You are not perfect, nobody is. Just as an event is just an event—feedback is just feedback. You like to get it, but may take it personally. It is one person's perspective. Digest it, don't internalize it. The more you focus on the negative, the more it will draw in other negative energy.

- Practice before you go into unchartered territories and remember that the goal is not perfection. Give yourself permission just to be okay.

- Give up the need to demand timeframes and deadlines from others. Instead, ask the other person the date they will be getting the information to you.

- Develop a plan on your calendar of 1-5 things you will do to move ahead through your Cloud of Ambiguity. (At least three steps have to be outside of your immediate work or safety zone area.)

- Give yourself a break—don't be so critical of yourself.

- When you achieve each area outside of your safety zone, check off those steps and celebrate those successes.

- Don't wait for the perfect opportunity. Resist the urge to judge an opportunity too quickly. Identify the positive points.

- Recognize that others with different drives do not see the level of detail that you do. They will need to depend on you for that thoroughness.

- Recognize that criticism can be based on a variety of perceptions. It is often an opinion.

- Recognize that some people talk about ideas to generate them. If you think they have just indicated what they want to do next, layer what you thought you heard. For example, "So, what I'm hearing you say is that you're going to do ____ by January 31?" They will confirm whether they are just generating ideas, verbalizing their thoughts, or confirming an action step.

Interacting with Conscientious Connie

If you interact with Conscientious Connie, understand that she needs information to make a decision. As a new supervisor, she wants and needs training. Ask her what holds her back, what information she needs, or what is the next step. These are questions that may help Conscientious Connie move through her Cloud of Ambiguity.

While Flexible Fran views Connie's need for the details as a waste of time or of procrastination in decision making, Connie wants to make sure she is making the right decision.

Her strength is that she is able to see the potential pitfalls of a situation, although this strength may be perceived as a weakness: looking at the potential problems rather than the opportunities. As she creates awareness about her level of conscientiousness, she learns that not everything needs to be or look perfect.

Connie inherently wants constructive feedback. Let her know what she has done well and what she could have done differently. She relies on this feedback for continuous improvement. However, it is critical to ask her if she wants the feedback that you provide to her.

SELF-REFLECTION MOMENT FOR CONSCIENTIOUS CONNIE

What if you didn't try to remove barriers before decision making?

Is perfection an issue?

How can mediocrity benefit you?

How do you react to feedback?

What if you asked yourself what's right with X, after you notice what needs to improved?

Summary

What does this all mean to navigate through your Cloud of Ambiguity? The more you understand yourself and grow your awareness of your natural motivators, the more effective you can be *who* you are, define where you are going, and understand how to interact with others—regardless of whether you relate to them or they are the opposite of you. This understanding about yourself and others carries you through life and during times of change.

You will find yourself relating to some characters and not others. For example, you may see parts of yourself in Conscientious Connie, Audacious Adam and Juggler Jane, but not Calm Chris. Still, you may have a relationship with or have contact with someone like Chris. It is to your benefit to understand what motivates others and the best ways to interact with them.

What do these characters have in common? They all are looking at the same thing differently. Their ability to meet on common ground is to understand:

- Everyone has ideas

- Everyone thinks, feels, and generates those ideas differently

- Everyone processes the ideas differently

- Everyone needs degrees of information on those ideas to move ahead

The more we think of each other's differences, the more we are the same. The secret is to discover how to balance the differences.

Everyone naturally gravitates toward that which motivates them and you use these motivators to live life and navigate change. You may not be able to change the natural way you approach life events but you can manage your motivators when they limit your progress.

In managing those motivators or needs, you can often get different results simply by managing that awareness and changing your approach. The Cloud of Ambiguity is a time to be open to different experiences. Changing your approach can:

- Generate a deeper and more effective sense of self and others
- Develop the path that you are on
- Emerge a previously untapped talent or enhance old ones
- Create a new vision for your future

Chapter Six

Navigating Without Awareness

Navigating through the Cloud of Ambiguity can be tricky. As we've learned with these characters, we navigate through change, with our natural motivators or needs. We gravitate to what we know—the natural way we navigate through life.

We emerge from our Clouds of Ambiguity when we are ready, or willing to let go of what has held us back. What holds us back may be an event, an assumption, a feeling, or what we anticipate might happen. We might not travel on a cross-country trip without a map or supplies; yet, we try to build our lives, select careers, and build businesses without first knowing our natural motivators. Creating awareness about those motivators, and those things that lay below the surface, gives us the greater knowledge to choose. Choose:

- Why we make the decisions we make about our lives;

- What makes up our natural needs; and

- What energizes us.

One cold winter day, Larry found himself between jobs. Larry had the natural ability to troubleshoot and identify why something didn't work. This same strength kept him circling in his Cloud of Ambiguity. He had a series of jobs but wasn't happy and felt isolated. When I asked him how he found the directions to our meeting place, he began to critique how there were no numbers on the buildings and how we were not between the two crossroads as the directions indicated.

Was it he who was on the crossroads? The numbers on the buildings were about four feet high—yet he became frustrated about the directions. He is innately wired to find errors or ways it could be improved. To him, the directions were not exacting enough. Through conversation, he said that he hates conflict and mentioned that he had a boss who was demeaning. He was motivated for perfection and he was sensitive to criticism. Something he said prompted me to probe at what point in his career was his boss demeaning. This negative experience he relayed occurred over seven years earlier. The emotion with which he spoke about this negative event was as if it had occurred yesterday.

We can all find something positive out of an otherwise negative situation if we ask ourselves what we have control over. Perhaps we stayed in the situation too long or we simply just needed to align our values to the environment we were working in. Perhaps we needed to learn something about ourselves or others. Perhaps it has nothing to do with us personally but we happen to be involved—involved as a conduit to help another's learning. For Larry he didn't let go of that feeling and allowed it to keep festering.

On a cold March day, I met a man quite like Spirited Sandy who went through a life transition. After his Sales Representative position was eliminated, he secured another job. He enjoyed the lifestyle and the many treasures his job brought him. He would articulate that he liked having all of the treasures and attention that his high-paying job afforded him. He was motivated by the acknowledgement he felt when he received compliments about those things he acquired. He rose to the top of his field quickly yet, when he got there, he was bored. He began to think of what really motivated him...and it simply was not his job any longer, but he got that innate need met (that acknowledgement).

He came to a point where other things in life, like family, became more important. He enjoyed his power, authority and things that he acquired. Yet, this life transition—a job loss—caused him to re-evaluate what was important. Climbing the corporate ladder was important to him. Attaining a six-figure income was important. Was it the ultimate goal that was important? Was there an importance in his journey?

Nice house, six or seven-figure salary, then what? Once that goal is achieved is there a sense of well-being?

For him, he couldn't articulate *who* he really was... what drove this man to be so focused on power, authority and things? Why was getting compliments or noticed for his sports car so important to him? When he got to the top of his field, where could he go from there?

Upon further discussion, he revealed that when he was little, he was placed in the special needs class because of the yearly examination scores he received were low. His parents knew that their child was intelligent and requested that the examiners talk with him one-on-one about the reading assignments. He scored at a high level. He wasn't a slow learner, after all, he just couldn't read the chalk board when he had the examination. He was tested for glasses, his grades improved and he was placed with the higher-level performers.

What impact did this event have on a child who innately needed acknowledgement and, as an adult, still needed to prove he was smart? Did he have an innate need for recognition of his ideas and did acknowledgement from others motivate him? Did one event have an impact on how he now navigated through his life?

If you are in an environment that doesn't support or fully express *who* you are, what are other alternatives? We often assume that there are no other environments that will yield what we have now—even though these assumptions often go untested.

One day, this gentleman met up with someone who mentioned a nonprofit organization that provided services to the underprivileged. He listened to a person he had just met and that person's stories of helping the underserved. Wow, he thought to himself, why am I so interested in helping others? I've been working in an industry that deals with widgets and things, yet I'm drawn to this nonprofit that provides services to people.

Who was this man—innately? What did he do well? Not

only was he articulate but he was also naturally talented at developing systems. He responded to his customers with great speed. He eloquently expressed himself and ideas. He could analyze a situation and construct a well-formed structure and process. Would the people in this industry embrace someone who had this natural ability even though he had no experience in that industry?

How would life be different if he created an awareness of what motivated him? What could happen if he let go of what others thought of him and allowed his natural talent within to emerge? Knowledge can be acquired. Natural talent is born and nurtured.

He started his own business and found that he needed the interaction with others, so he found a way to expand his nonprofit business to get that need met. He now enjoys a balance between work, family, and is continuously focused on his vision for his future.

SELF-REFLECTION MOMENT

Have you been putting energy into proving to others how accomplished you are?

How much energy do you place in what you perceive as negative events?

What is good or valuable about those events?

Are you putting energy into something that occurred many years, months, or days earlier?

Ask yourself: What's really important to you right now? Write down all that is important to you.

CHAPTER SEVEN

LET ME INTRODUCE YOU TO THE INNER CRITIC AND OUTER CRITIC

One of the greatest hurdles to navigate through your Cloud of Ambiguity and live a desired life is the inner and outer critics. The critics can be the result of motivators you try to get met. When you experience change, especially unanticipated change, those motivators turn into needs and go into overdrive and, thus, your inner and outer critics can become stronger if uncontrolled.

The inner critic is the part of you that places limitations in your thinking and behavior. It lies beneath, those internal discussions you have with yourself. It is a mechanism that we learned about as children when we learned about right or wrong, good or bad, and this or that. The inner critic involves judgment, approval, and tells us we're not good enough. But when is good, good enough? The inner critic gives rise to the outer critic.

The outer critic is what you say or do on the outside that is observed and is an extension to what you might say to yourself on the inside.

The inner and outer critics are present to different degrees and are displayed differently depending on what motivates us. As you can see with each character, their motivators have an impact on how their inner critic and outer critic are represented. Additionally, you can see the inner and outer critic in action to get their motivators met.

Character	Needs	Inner Critic Conversation or Behavior	Outer Critic Conversation or Behavior
Harmonious Hazel	Needs harmony and may avoid or prevent conflict	"Why did you get criticized for that project?" If you did better, there would not be disagreement! Feels she let herself or the team down.	Criticizes others who disagree with her. Stressed and frustrated by debate or disagreement. May shut down from the conversation or walk away. Takes small steps or risks to navigate the change.
Audacious Adam	Needs debate, challenge and independence over environment and decisions. Needs his ideas implemented.	"Why didn't you get the results?" "Why didn't you reach your goal?" "Why do I need to discuss it with you?"	May hear him say, "If your ideas were any good, you would stand up for them!" May resist decisions or ideas that aren't his and seeks out debate and argument. Is results-oriented and makes or fills in gaps with assumptions.
Analytical Ann	Needs time alone to think and figure things out for herself	"You need to be thoughtful about whatever you say!" "You should be able to figure this out by yourself."	Criticizes others for talking off the cuff or thinking aloud. May keep her thoughts to herself. Responds with short answers.

Character	Needs	Inner Critic Conversation or Behavior	Outer Critic Conversation or Behavior
Spirited Sandy	Needs acknowledgement and group interaction to generate ideas	"Why weren't you able to persuade them?" "You need to present yourself well."	May criticize others who are not persuaded by her ideas or those who process their thoughts on the inside. Quick to respond and verbalizes to resolve the change
Calm Chris	Needs order, process and time to change	"There should be an order—this process is inefficient—strive for efficiencies!"	Becomes frustrated with others when a process is interrupted or there is not a structure. Seeks out the process or next steps.
Juggler Jane	Needs and seeks out variety and quick resolution	"You can do it all!" "You should be able to do it all!"	Denounces people who don't think or move as fast. Cuts off people's conversations and stops listening. Appears impatient or wants her information quickly.
Connscientious Connie	Need for perfection and structure	Is critical of herself or attacks herself when she gets something wrong.	Criticizes others for errors. Asks questions to seek information.
Flexible Fran	Need for freedom and flexibility	Fran's inner critic may be represented as beating herself up for not achieving results, looking bad in front of others or not being organized.	Faults people who are too politically correct, exacting, process focused or who didn't get result as she thought they should. Is casual in conversation and doesn't like it when others are too formal.

What is seen as criticism on the outside, may be a peek into your inner critic. Your outer critic can be an extension of what you need. For example, if Analytical Ann criticizes Spirited Sandy for talking aloud about her ideas without thinking about them inside, Ann's inner critic is saying, Think about what you say before you say it. Her outer critic sounds off by criticizing Sandy for not being careful in what Sandy communicates. Ann needs to think things through carefully (Ann's needs) and criticizes others who may talk out loud to generate ideas (Ann's outer critic).

In order to navigate change, however, it is important to calm the inner and outer critics. Acceptance is the key. Accept what naturally motivates you *and* others and understand that when people are navigating change, there is a heightened push to get those motivators or needs met. In another example, Juggler Jane wants to quickly get results or move through change rapidly. Calm Chris needs time to create a process or think through change. Imagine if both Jane and Chris worked in the same organization experiencing a merger. Chris needs time to absorb the change, while Jane needs to resolve or move quickly through it. Each wants to get their needs met and their inner and outer critics, if left unmanaged, can increase an already stressful event.

When managed, the inner critic can be a positive survival mechanism. When we're children, our parents teach us lessons that stay with us—if I touch the stove, I'll get burned; I should disinfect a cut so it doesn't get infected; and I shouldn't talk to strangers. These behaviors emerge as our survival mechanisms yet they can become our limiters if taken to extremes or left untested. They become part of our assumption systems that exist just below the surface yet a very real part of our decision-making process and mode of operation.

If these modes of operation are left untested, they can turn these mechanisms into barriers that prevent us from being who we are and doing work using our natural motivators. As children, we used those experiences to judge whether someone was a stranger or gauge whether you were behaving appropriately in the restaurant. These lessons help us to survive, but, as adults, they can limit our success. If we never test the "don't talk to strangers" assumption, we may never talk to them even though we may be have a natural motivation to do so. Some of the inner critic conversations can keep you striving for improvement but the inner critic needs to be restrained and understood.

SELF-REFLECTION MOMENT

Think of the change you are going through right now and think about the following questions:

When or where does your inner critic show up?

If you are criticizing others, is it a reflection of what you see or expect of yourself?

Do you understand how you are motivated and the impact it is having on your moving with and through change?

What is the inner critic saying to you about changes you want/need to make?

How are your motivators impacting your ability to move through change?

CHAPTER EIGHT

CHANGE HAPPENS

Early in my career, I thought I was prepared for everything. I would go to school, get an education, work hard, get a great job and get promoted. Simple equation. Driven toward my career goals, I was unaware of my natural motivators, focused on the immediate environment and worked incredible hours to get that promotion.

Up to this point, I was accustomed to hard work, funded my education, worked full time, and planned a wedding. Finally, I landed a job I had strived to secure. So here I was in a relatively new job, worked many hours to get a promotion yet there was this nagging feeling. The lump I'd found behind my ear ten months earlier was still there. A specialist would deliver the malignant news (a life event placing me in my Cloud of Ambiguity.) My first thought was, "How am I going to continue to work all of these hours to get that job and go through treatment?" Did I need to listen to something else?

At about the same time, a temporary replacement for the top job that I'd been working so hard to get was brought in to the Company. Since this individual was transitioning to a new role in the company but at a different branch and that position had not yet been vacated, she was temporarily placed at my location. Admittedly, I felt a bit deflated that the decision was made to place her there, but viewed this arrangement as an opportunity to learn from her. How interesting that a person was placed in a lead role while I was learning a new lesson about life.

Over the next five weeks, there was a series of radiation treatments. Relieved there was someone in the lead role, I worked through this life priority and what was really important to me—my healing.

A change began to happen not only in the work environment, but for me personally. I realized that I didn't have to do it all. In fact, I couldn't do it all. I discovered the art of delegation and managed an urgent need to respond to everything. It was a relief to release the priority I placed on work. It also gave others the opportunity to grow in their own way.

A very short time later, I was promoted. However, I needed to learn the art of delegation before that transition to the role. Strange, how change happens. As humans, we try to explain why change occurs and answers are not always immediate. Retrospect and distance from events can bring understanding of the positive impact these events have on our transformation.

Change happens but we need to ask ourselves these questions before we can navigate through it:

SELF-REFLECTION MOMENT

Is there change that is occurring or has occurred that stopped you from your routine?

Do you try or are you trying to control what is happening?

Which motivators get in the way of what's important?

Is there an inner critic that needs to be tamed?

What is really important?

Do you just sit by and watch change happen or try to make it happen your way?

Do you try to do everything?

What assumptions do you make about things, people, situations, and yourself?

What is the bigger picture?

Chapter Nine

Examining Your Life's Cycles

L̲ike a wheel on a bicycle, life goes round and round and change occurs daily. As a child, I rode along the sidewalk as the wind breezed through my long hair and the warm, bright sun beat on my face when all of a sudden... WAMM! My pant leg got jammed into the chain of the bike. Do you remember coasting along and an event occurred giving you pause to think about your path in life?

Every so often your pant leg gets caught in that chain. As you look at events that have occurred, think about the dates, years or intervals associated with those events. Chart your life listing all of the positive events as well as the challenging times. For example, when you chart your lifeline, do you notice a certain month or interval of time that becomes apparent?

Over time, you may see patterns or cycles emerging. If you identify a negative event that occurs, when did your next positive event occur? And vice versa.

When you identify your cycle times, you begin to

create a greater awareness about your emerging times and times where you may want to move with the change. What are your cycle times?

To identify your life's cycles, take a look at your life timeline. Begin by identifying the date of your earliest childhood memory. Identify all of the significant events (graduation, new job, former jobs ending, significant life events, losses, marriages, divorces, recoveries, etc.) Then, list the month and year each event began and/or when they ended. Once you have filled in your life's timeline, reflect on the questions that follow.

Example:

Born   Today's Date

SELF REFLECTION MOMENT

Are there life events that had positive and/or negative impacts on your life?

Do you see any trends or patterns in the months or years of health issues, relationships, promotions, demotions, deaths, or other significant change? Do any dates, intervals, numbers, or issues keep surfacing?

Do similar issues or lessons keep appearing around the same times?

Is the change you experience now just the normal course of when change occurs for you?

How are these changes related to your strengths or your weaknesses and/or limitations?

During times of change, how do approach it (push through it, take it on and accommodate others, systematically work through it, take on the stress of making the perfect choices?)

Is there a pattern that emerges when you experience significant change in your life?

Do events that seem negative later turn into positives?

Do you resist change?

How will new knowledge about your cycles help you navigate change?

PHASE 2:

FINDING POSSIBILITIES

CHAPTER TEN

THE ART OF LETTING GO!

Finding new possibilities can be a daunting task. Yet, it is when you let go, that new worlds or opportunities can emerge.

LeeAnn is a professional trainer in classroom-style training who was laid off from her job. For over a year, she looked for work before she decided to freelance. She learned about a different kind of training and began to see a lot of work in this new experiential learning area where she worked with people outside of the traditional classroom setting. Whenever she landed work on the classroom-style training she used to do, the evaluations from the participants were neutral to average. How could that be? She had received exceptional reviews during her career. She didn't understand why she received neutral to average reviews now.

Many agonizing sessions later, LeeAnn left behind her classroom-style training and focused on this new experiential training and she began to see a change: the participant's evaluations were exceptional. LeeAnn saw a lot of herself in Spirited Sandy and Conscientious Connie. She naturally connected with others, was precise in her work and gained confidence in what she knew. But did that precision and comfortableness in what she knew prevent her from moving much quicker into this new experiential learning instead of doing something she had known?

Through her transition, LeeAnn decided that she needed to embrace this new delivery of training.

LeeAnn is learning about her Cloud of Ambiguity and how to move beyond it. Her Cloud was the confusion she experienced when she tried to do the same classroom-style training and expected rave reviews. It was time for her to do something different and she was hanging on to what was comfortable yet, she was receiving lower evaluation (messages) from something she used to excel in.

Everyone proceeds through their Cloud of Ambiguity at their own pace. Fast to you may be slow to others. Slow to you, may be fast to others. But judgment on how fast is fast and is fast good may keep you in your Cloud. Honor the place where you are today—wherever that place may be. You are who you are in the place you are. At a point that you determine, there is a time to let go of what was and begin to invite what can be.

Isn't it interesting how spring brings the rain? How it washes away the salt and debris from the roads to make way for new sprouts and beginnings so effortlessly? Imagine for a moment staying in the late winter weather. Overcast and cold. When we choose to stay in our Cloud of Ambiguity, it is like remaining in the damp days of winter.

We gravitate toward those things that are within our safety zones, that are familiar to us, that which we know. But as we progress through the Cloud of Ambiguity, we begin to take action on what can be.

How much energy do you put into an event? It has been said, an event is just an event. "It is what it is." It happened, learn from it, and let it go. Yet we hang on to it because we don't know what will happen.

When a person has a natural ability to see errors or what could be better and experience what they see as a negative event, they will have a natural tendency to rerun that negative experience and how they were wrong or wronged. If the person doesn't like the conflict they experienced, they will obsess over it, and place a significant amount of energy into it. They may not even attempt something new for fear of failure. Or if the person barrels through change without thought, it may prevent real results because they may not reflect or think it through. These natural motivators, though, can keep us stuck if not managed.

How do you let it go?

Do you have a negative event that keeps you from living the life you want to lead? Are you operating out of a fear of what might happen? How do you let it go?

Write down that event on a piece of paper. Write your deepest thoughts, feelings and what that event changed in your life both the good and the bad.

Once you write down that event, tear it up or destroy it. Physically get it out of your space and allow yourself ceremoniously to let it go.

People who have experienced a significant life event, usually have an article of clothing, logo of the organization or some other reminder. They might also have a cologne or perfume that reminds them of the place or certain relationship. When they take that item and write a note to themselves destroying the note or article of clothing, they have mentally allowed themselves to bring an end to that event. Likewise, when they change their cologne or perfume, they are starting anew.

This practical exercise helps an individual take a much-needed step to start to move out of their Cloud of Ambiguity and into new possibilities. While this one exercise may not completely allow that person to let go, it is certainly a start to navigate change. Sometimes, it takes baby steps to get to where you want to be.

Letting go is about identifying what doesn't work anymore and making a different choice. When you have the ability to let it go and integrate your experience into your life, you're ready to move on to the next phase: Thinking of possibilities.

Self-Reflection Moment

Is the action you take producing results that will get you to your desired future?

Which way are you moving: forward, backward, or standing still?

Are you doing things you have always done or have done before? Is there something you would like to do differently?

Is there a balance between the work that you do and the life that you lead outside of work?

Are you in a performance trap?

How are you relating to others?

Do you forge your agenda?

Is pleasing others more important than pleasing yourself?

Is your current environment energizing or de-energizing you?

Is there a fear or behavior you want to let go of?

What one step can you take to move ahead?

CHAPTER ELEVEN

WHAT'S POSSIBLE?

If you have successfully worked through the exercise in Chapter 10, you may be ready to read further. But if you're not ready, you may want to come to this next section at a later date when you have resolved what no longer works for you. Life is full of choices. What are your choices to move forward?

You'll know you're ready when you can answer these questions. Write down your answers to the questions below:

1. What are your natural needs? What motivates you?

2. What are the insights you developed from reading about the characters or situations?

3. What do you need in order to let go of an undesirable or negative event or situation? How much energy do you place into events that have already happened?

4. Describe your desired future. What does it look like and who is involved? How are you feeling there? What are you thinking while in your desired future? Draw a picture of it or describe what it looks like in words.

5. What one positive step can you take to move closer to your desired future? (It doesn't have to be a big step, maybe it's a little step or series of steps.) Write down each of these steps.

When you complete this exercise, it is important for you to post your desired future in the area you live. This will be the future you work toward.

Each day, write down a step on your calendar that moves you closer to that desired future. Keep this exercise to build on as you read through Vision Development and Action Planning.

CHAPTER 12

FAITH IN THE CLOUD

*Faith gives you the courage, calmness and confidence
to reveal the authentic you.*

While in the Cloud of Ambiguity, some days will be better than others. There will be times you think and feel positive about the possibilities. Yet, there will be other days where you don't see the results you want and feel sad or consumed in negative thought.

When you converse with people who have navigated much change in their life, one thing stands out during the hard times...faith. Faith that things will get better. I'm not referring to an organized religion, rather something greater than all of humankind. Some people will call it a belief in God, others will call it Spirit, still others call it faith...a belief in something greater than yourself at work for your higher good. We'll call it faith for now.

Faith during transition takes on a certain meaning for everyone. If you know and believe that there is a reason you may not see at the moment, but know that you are where you are for a reason, then this faith allows you to let go of what happened, see the possibilities, allow people and ideas in, and provide courage to allow the authentic you to emerge.

At first, I wondered, Who wants to read an entire chapter on faith in transition? Then, I was asked on three different occasions within a short span of each other... Are you going to include something in your book about faith? Well, it didn't take a tire iron this time...here's an entire section on faith in transition!

Let's look at faith in a different way wherein there is meaning in the word itself.

> **F**orthrightness
>
> **A**cceptance
>
> **I**nsight
>
> **T**rust
>
> **H**onesty

The first step to have faith is forthrightness.

Forthrightness means being direct. While you navigate change, there are times you will want to avoid starting something new because of what others will say, think, or what you allow your inner critic to tell you.

Forthrightness allows you to be direct with yourself, create awareness about your natural motivators, and manage these innate needs. It allows you to embrace new ways of thinking and gives yourself permission to be authentic.

For example, if Harmonious Hazel never acknowledges her natural need to avoid conflict with others or that conflict gives her stress, forthrightness is not present—a key ingredient in faith that helps navigate transition toward transformation. She may experience situations or environments where she is in constant debate, hence not getting her natural needs met.

Forthrightness allows you to embrace your choice over what you think and what you do based on what you want for your future. Forthrightness gives you the directness needed to determine who you are and living in alignment with it.

The second step to have faith is Acceptance.

Acceptance allows you to integrate your experiences into your life as well as to accept others. For example, if Adam chooses not to accept his downsizing and chooses to debate the decision of his employer, he is not in acceptance. He, in essence, has not integrated his experience so that he can turn the event into a positive aspect of his life. While he tries to get his need for debate met, he prohibits his talent for creating ideas from emerging sooner. While it may not have been his choice to leave the company, he has an opportunity to be something even greater. Adam had thoughts that he worked better independently than in his team-oriented company culture. He can maximize his true self by transitioning to a new environment and better managing those natural motivators. When Adam felt frustrated by working in a team-oriented environment, his inner voice was telling him that he was not getting his innate needs or motivators met. He would have been energized if he was getting his motivators met.

There are reasons why you experience each event

every day. Faith is accepting that everything, including who you are, develops in its perfect order.

The third step to have faith in transition is Insight.

Insight involves clarity. You align yourself with faith when you have clarity in your vision for your future. Clarity of purpose comes when you have forthrightness to identify your innate talents and strengths, acceptance of self and others, and develop a clear understanding of your purpose.

Do you try to be someone you inherently are not? How do you know? If you don't feel good about what you are doing or the life you are living, you may not have clarity of your purpose. You may be misaligned in your life, the environment you live, or resisting the change.

To help create insight into your purpose, ask:

- What are your innate strengths and/or talents?

- What do you want to contribute—your family, your community, society, and the world?

- What do you want to be remembered for?

- Are you living in alignment with what you want to be remembered for?

As you cultivate insight into your purpose, accept who you innately are and manage your motivators, you can create alignment with your purpose.

The fourth step to have faith in transition is Trust.

Trust involves conviction that everything is constantly aligning and evolving. The first time you rode a bike, you were apprehensive. Do you remember how you felt the first time you got your training wheels off of your bike? You didn't trust that you could ride that bike and not fall. Transition is like getting your training wheels off of your bike. You don't trust that which you know and may have fear with those things that are unclear or undefined. Everything seems different yet everything you have experienced has prepared you for this very moment. You have to trust that you continue to build on your foundation.

Aligning in faith is trusting that you can ride that bike. You may fall off, but you'll get up again and learn something new in the process.

What is a theme that you see or think of yourself throughout your life that makes you feel good?

Can others see the changes you are making (or not making) because of the circumstances and have tried to tell you? Are you listening to those messages?

Do you feel good about a change you're making but don't trust that change? For example, Michael left his executive position and began his own company. It took some time, but he began to see more business coming his way. In fact, he was energized by getting the business and growing it. The work was steady, he got more business, yet he didn't trust the change. There were times where he gravitated toward finding another corporate position working for someone else—although he was not excited about that option. It was safe. He didn't trust that the changes he made were in perfect alignment because he was comparing the former revenue he made in his established company with the revenue he generated in his new company and his results were not immediate. Was he naturally wired for immediate results perhaps?

Having faith involves trust: that the emerging path is more in alignment with your long-term purpose, your innate motivators, your needs and the life you want to lead.

Comfortably Uncomfortable

Comfortably uncomfortable is the place you are in when you seemingly take action but the action does not produce results you can see. It's that place where you have faith that there is a reason for you to be in the place at that moment.

Is being in the moment a challenge for you? That is, do you have difficulty being fully present in a situation without thinking about the next step or the next result? Do you have difficulty savoring the moment, the feeling, and the environment? Being?

It is an acknowledgement when you're in a comfortably uncomfortable space that creates an empowered feeling and sense of well-being.

A simple example of being comfortably uncomfortable comes when you're stuck in traffic. Certainly, you want to get to your appointment on time but you're stuck in traffic. You do not see the results you want (to get to your appointment on time.) When you are in control of how you react to a situation, how you feel, and what you think about you are comfortably uncomfortable. You are at peace with the place you are in. In this case, you find positive things to engage your thoughts and are thankful not to be involved in the fender bender ahead.

Transition is about faith: faith in yourself; faith in being comfortably uncomfortable, faith in the circumstances; faith in the perfect balance of life, and a deeper faith in something greater than yourself at work.

The fifth step to have faith in transition is Honesty.

People who are diagnosed with cancer often say that they don't want anyone to know they have it. For a variety of reasons, there is a period of time where they want to assume the experience alone. Yet, when they come to terms and are honest with others about where they are in their treatment and how they feel, they find that they can transition through the treatment with much more ease rather than focus on the dis-ease alone.

For example, when I received news of a malignancy, I felt that I could not let anybody know that I had the "C" word. Would I not get a promotion because they didn't feel I could handle it? As odd as this sounds to me now, I thought that I somehow failed. It wasn't until much later that I realized the infinite power within.

During this health transition, I became open to messages that I'd received, allowed others to know about my health challenge, and realized that it was not about being weak. I leaned on others when speaking or swallowing became difficult because of the treatments. I had to be honest with myself on my limitations. It was not about what others think or say or do. It is about the strength within to make the changes, to hear the messages, and to accept the learning. It was only much later that I would realize that sharing my experiences would inspire them. By not sharing, I was not giving others an opportunity to learn from my experience.

In your transition, you hear or see messages that guide you. Faith, especially in transition, allows us to know there is a deeper positive meaning. Sometimes our life's events are not even about us but the impact the events have on others.

Faith is to know that people are placed in your path. It may not be what we need to learn rather what they will learn and an element in being able to manage being comfortably uncomfortable.

Do you need to hear messages several times before becoming aware of them? Do you just need to learn to "be?" Do you need to learn the patience to be where you are, when you are and be at peace within that and every moment?

What are messages? Did you ever receive a call and wonder, "why is that person calling me?" It could be a question from someone unexpected. It could be a person wanting to tell you about another opportunity but one that initially you never thought of, one that you can't immediately see yourself pursue. It could be a person you met and wondered how odd that I met them today. These are all potential messages, potential paths you can take, potential windows of opportunities. They may not align with where you are today, but stop. Give them some thought. It may not be what you want, but it may be an opportunity you can try in the meantime to get you one step closer to your authentic or true self.

All too often, we don't consider the potential messages.

These messages are part of faith. The faith that we need to align ourselves to accept that which we ask for and, what we ask for will be delivered in a way that is for our higher good. Perhaps we need to go through what we need to go through to:

- Work outside of our safety zones;

- Find our purpose and align ourselves to that purpose;

- Explore who we really are and what really motivates us;

- Be honest about our authentic identity;

- Learn to listen to others or to ourselves.

- Find patience with being.

- Be...just be in the moment.

Faith comes in knowing that something—a greater power than you, knows something that you don't know. Wanting to know, to control, can be your safety zone emerging. Do you think Audacious Adam or Conscientious Connie would like to know? Sure they would. But faith comes in knowing that you don't know and being comfortably uncomfortable in that place.

Self-Reflection Moment

What is your inner voice saying?

What is the real issue?

What's important?

Why would you say no?

What are you saying no to?

Why would you say yes?

What are you saying yes to?

Are you looking at the opportunity?

Is operating out of fear an issue?

What are you gravitating toward? Is it safety, security, prestige or other?

Are you being who you truly are with a level of awareness?

Are you trying to mold yourself into what someone else or an environment wants?

Is there an opportunity to reflect who you are today and who you want to become?

What lessons have you had to learn about yourself when others were placed in your path?

How can you become more comfortably uncomfortable when events present themselves?

CHAPTER THIRTEEN

PROFESSIONAL PERFECTIONISM

No matter your role, Professional Perfectionism can keep you from discovering your innate self. Professional perfectionism is where you strive for expert precision in your field at times at the expense of other areas in your life. It is also when you place yourself with strong identity in what you do.

For example, stay-at-home mothers and fathers may align themselves with Professional Perfectionism. When their children grow up, the parents are outside of their role as caregiver. This Professional Perfectionism can interfere with your ability to find your true or new path in life. It can keep you so focused on what you do rather than *who* you are that you don't see the messages that hide in your peripheral vision. You get in the way of exploring all of the possibilities.

Your identity can cause you to be blinded by alternatives and of the possibilities. For example, you worked hard in your career and even harder to for promotions. One day, an event occurs. Perhaps your company goes bankrupt and now you discover that something needs to change. You're in the thick of your Cloud of Ambiguity and you have much knowledge about your area of expertise yet it seems impossible to do something else in your life. What makes you different? What are your talents? Do you have to do what you have always done?

These are important questions to ask yourself in order to move on to a different place in life. For your own personal growth, it is important when to realize that your professional perfectionism prevents you from venturing into other areas outside of your safety zone of knowledge. You feel safe when you continue to do what you have always done.

SELF-REFLECTION MOMENT

Reflect on the questions below answering yes or no. Look at the key to see if Professional Perfectionism is present.

	YES	No
Are you in transition and don't share it with others because you are concerned with how you may be perceived?		
Is finding another or different role difficult for you?		
Do you place an emphasis on what others may think in changing your role?		
Do you strive to be perfect in the role you do or have done?		
When you meet someone, do you find that one of the first things you mention is the role you hold or your title?		

	YES	NO
Are you or have you been consumed with the role that you do or are in?		
Do you reject help in your work because only you can do it the best?		
TOTAL THE NUMBER OF YES ANSWERS		

KEY TO THE NUMBER OF YES ANSWERS

1-2 = You may need to change an area of your life to keep it balanced.

3 or More = You may need to take active steps to align your life with who you are and what you do.

CHAPTER FOURTEEN

BALANCE AND YOUR AUTHENTIC SELF

As mentioned in Professional Perfectionism, your identity can be lost with the job you do. Stay-at-home moms or dads can lose their identities in their children. Professionals and workers can lose their identities in the work they do. The job or role becomes who you are rather than what you do, which is different from doing work in alignment with who you are. When you lose your role, a serious accident occurs or other event prompting change, you begin to then reprioritize and realize: Who are you really? What makes you who you are? Are you getting all that motivates you met? Are you feeling energized or de-energized? What's really important in life?

John had radiation to his neck for a cancerous node and had difficulty speaking, swallowing, and eating, but rarely took time off of work. He spent incredible hours at work—a Professional Perfectionist. He set career goals but often had difficulty standing up for himself. He was an accommodator. He took on more and more and more work and family projects. He was treated with radiation to his neck and throat area—the very area that would allow him to speak up for himself. Saying no when he had too much work was difficult for him.

The treatments made John devoid of energy. This energy drain forced him to look at what he could and could not do. For that period of time, he had to focus on what was really important. He balanced his health and professional time and work was not as important. He learned that not all requests had to be completed immediately. He had much in common with Juggler Jane who always responded with urgency. He learned that other people accepted schedule changes. More importantly, he learned to let go of the work so that he could spend time on healing. He received a push, his illness: a gift really, to help him transition. It helped him balance his motivators and discover an enriched life.

Discovering who you are, and where your strengths, weaknesses and relationships lie, is the catalyst to manage your natural motivators, invite balance, and understand messages that may come to you. Reflection may also be helpful in shifting from a performance- and achievement-driven place to aligning with inner peace and confidence in your authentic self.

Whether you have physical challenges, experience organizational change, or discover other transformational times, the real issue is to identify what is really going on personally. Each of us reacts to change differently based on our learned behaviors, our experiences and what makes us unique—our motivators. Embracing differences and understanding the dynamics of those unique needs help you to communicate and to develop more effective relationships and find your purpose.

Creating your transformation, however, takes courage. This courage comes in two forms: (1) courage to allow space for others to adjust to the change; and (2) courage to allow yourself to embrace change.

Authentic Self

As the climate changes, especially in the winter months, we put on mittens, boots, hats and masks that will protect us from the elements of the cold harsh winter. We adapt to our surroundings. Illness, job change or other losses can bring a new wave of change, and we react by putting on those mittens to comfort us. We go to our natural motivators. As we've seen with John, illness can mask deeper, unresolved issues and the body has a way of pushing out a more authentic self.

When you go through an event or change, you often want to hold on to things as if those things will serve a purpose. Yet, it is when you let go and reveal what lay beneath those masks, you invite new things into your life allowing a more authentic self to emerge.

SELF-REFLECTION MOMENT

Are you on a performance- or achievement-driven tread-mill?

Do you need to balance your life to reveal the authentic you?

Where in your life do you need more balance?

Is there a mask that you developed that may be holding you back?

Do you let people see what you want them to see?

In doing work or living life in alignment with who you are, what if you asked yourself—what do I want from *all* areas of my life?

Do you allow space for others to adjust to changes you are making?

CHAPTER FIFTEEN

GAINING PERSPECTIVE

At the beginning of radiation therapy, my energy level was stable, so on one September morning, I drove myself to work. It was a particularly sunny September morning. The trees seemed greener, the sky bluer and the clouds fluffier....yeah, fluffier. Stay with me here...

You see, this event caused my perspective to change. I began to notice the simple things in life. I began to learn what was really important.

When an event occurs, it can shift our thinking for the positive or the negative. We have a choice on which viewpoint we embrace.

Lucy, a president of a successful company, could be described as ambitious, articulate and responding with urgency to her customers. While she was naturally good at responding to pressures, she got on the treadmill of *always* responding to her environment, sometimes at the risk of her own ideas, satisfaction or time. She was asked what stages she went through during her experience with breast cancer. For her, she realized that she

113

had been in denial about an event that occurred many years earlier.

Lucy reflected on her cancer's location and how much she denied her femininity. Her past life of abuse invaded her and now she had to deal with that reality. The cancer event brought to light a deeper unresolved issue. She began to realize an internal peace that the past event didn't define her, rather it was an event she needed to release. She was okay, it was okay, and letting go of what happened and acceptance of it brought peace.

Like her experience, Lucy learned that she needed to acknowledge how she felt and what she wanted. The word no was not in her vocabulary. How others would think and feel was her priority and she put herself last. It was the power of her own acceptance that allowed her to reshape who she was, what she did, and how she reacted (or didn't react) to her environment. She let go of being all things to all people and focused on the kind of life she wanted. She recognized that she felt pushed by others to accept traditional treatment when she thought about alternative forms of treatment for her disease. It was then she took responsibility for everything that was about to happen to her and made the decisions that were right for her, her relationships and her treatment.

Interestingly, Lucy recalls taking on everyone else's tribulations very deeply but now was fighting for a different cause. The career didn't seem to be as important and reaction to the change that was happening at work wasn't as important. She learned to let go of the level of importance she placed on work issues because in the whole realm of life, they seemed small and not something for which she wanted to be remembered. She let go of her Professional Perfectionism.

Lucy began to have clarity: Clarity of simple pleasures of daily life, the preciousness of her family and relationships, and the importance of examining her strengths. She aligned with a deeper faith. There is an old saying that says, 10 percent is what happens to you and 90 percent is how you react to it. Lucy began to understand what that meant. For Lucy, the only focus during this time was wellness. Spirituality took on a new and different meaning. For her, the family unit became stronger and her spirituality became predominant.

Self-Reflection Moment

Do you take on the problems of others?

What is the way to have others help?

Was there an event that gave you new perspective?

How can you gain perspective?

What did you learn?

CHAPTER SIXTEEN

CONSIDER THE UNCONSIDERED

Many of my childhood vacations were spent on a family farm. One summer afternoon, I learned how to navigate the 80 acres with a home-made minibike my brother put together. He had recently changed the gears wherein the accelerator was not the de-accelerator and vice versa. My older sister wanted a turn on the mini-bike. While I attempted to share with her the change that had been made to the accelerator, she waved her hands quickly dismissing my input. Well, she took off and in her haste had accelerated too fast and crashed into the chicken coop with a nasty jolt.

How often do we not consider the unconsidered or move ahead with assumptions that what once worked, will continue to work the same way?

It takes running into a chicken coop for much-needed change to occur or for people to see a different way of doing and being. By changing one small element, you could go in a new unconsidered direction, hopefully not by accident.

Take the horse harness industry. Before automobile manufacturing, the horse harness industry was a thriving business. Then, came the horseless carriage. Was the revolutionary automobile the tire iron story for the harness industry?

How did that change affect them? How did it change the workforce? If they limited themselves, would they have survived?

What new markets could they have developed? Could seatbelts been made of leather? Could they shift to leather seats?

Considering the possibilities of change and working in ambiguity is not easy, especially if there is not a plan.

It is not what a plan says, but what it does. Working out of ambiguity can become clearer when you begin to develop the vision and purpose and work in alignment with it. It becomes clear to you that Plan A is not the plan that works best. Suddenly, Plan B starts to work and you take steps toward a path different than what you expected. But to do that, you have to think about things you ordinarily would have not considered.

During ambiguity you may see trends or messages at work. You may see those messages from what is coming in your path or from people placed in your path, or from your inner voice that seems to get confirmed or gets louder. Listen to them. Consider the unconsidered.

Self-Reflection Moment

Can you have a Plan A *and* B?

Has someone mentioned a Plan B, but you quickly dismissed it?

What have you considered?

Is there something that hasn't been considered?

How often do you hear a message before you incorporate it?

Are you progressing the way you always have and is it providing good situations, feelings, relationships, and results?

CHAPTER SEVENTEEN

ASSUMPTION SYSTEMS

We often experience life, make assumptions and develop our belief systems based on those experiences. Assumptions from our experiences are a part of us that come from who we innately are. We often don't take the time to test those assumptions or belief systems. Is how we're motivated impacting our ability to test our assumption systems?

Let's take bottled water as an example. In the 1960s, who would have thought that people could make a profit off of something that was free! Yet, every day, we allow our assumptions and beliefs to go untested.

By not testing assumptions, there could be a missed opportunity. In this fast-changing world, what might have worked yesterday, may not work today. For example, upcoming generations have always known about the internet: instant messaging, instant information, and instant service. The very nature of the changing world is moving so fast that our assumption systems are impacted.

Why is it important to test our assumptions? If we write down our assumptions and have them in front of us, we create an awareness about them. We can then re-read them to see how and if our assumptions change.

When you say I think he's angry, I think she meant this or that, I can't make money at doing X, or I will never attain X, ask yourself, "how do I know?" Is there an assumption? Are beliefs causing you to place these barriers in your path? Are you naturally motivated to look at all the barriers before saying yes or taking action? How does your safety zone impact your assumptions?

Testing assumptions allows you the power to create: create possibilities. Without testing those assumptions, you may be resisting possibilities. Do you like everything about the world you live in? If not, you have the power to create a new world or different dimension of how you live your life.

Take a moment to list all of your assumptions. When you meet with someone, ask yourself, am I making judgments based on assumptions? Am I assuming through what I want to make or not make happen?

For example, Audacious Adam likes ideas, mostly his ideas. When he draws a conclusion, he may look at the information that supports his conclusion. In this case, he is casting aside other information that doesn't support his idea. In essence, he is trying to get his need for his idea met.

It is interesting how often we let our mental models, those perceptions we form from past experiences, affect how we react to future events. We worry about things that haven't happened yet or we anticipate happening. We react.

One day, a human resource executive in the hospitality industry hired a recruiter. The recruiter had previously worked in the education industry. The human resource executive received resistance from other peers for hiring the recruiter because the recruiter didn't have a hospitality background. But, the recruiter naturally connected with people, had a high response to time pressures, and had a history for great follow up and follow through on her work. Within six months the recruiter brought down the number of open positions in a branch with over 80% turnover and 40 openings to zero openings. She cut turnover in half. She could learn the industry but she already had the natural ability to approach the job in a way that got results.

The human resource executive worked against her peer's assumption systems and hired someone out of the industry but someone who had the natural ability to connect with others. It resulted in real savings to the company.

How often do assumption systems and those mental models you have about what should be, keep you from making the best decisions?

SELF-REFLECTION MOMENT

When have you observed things and reacted without all of the information and/or with assumption?

What have other's said about you? What do you think they mean by that? Is there something you assumed to come to that conclusion?

Think of a recent time you had a strong reaction? What were you reacting to?

What's important about testing your assumption systems?

Is what you are viewing fact or an assumption?

Are you making assumptions about a relationship? On a future career? On the next step you need to take?

Think of an area or situation you're dealing with where you want different results. What one assumption or belief can you change that would help you in living your desired future?

CHAPTER EIGHTEEN

THIS OR THAT?

Many people have a need to live in a world of good or bad, right or wrong. As a society, we think in terms of win or lose. Does it have to be win or lose, or right or wrong? Are there elements of both? Why is it, we look at good or bad or this or that? We never seem to look at the AND: this AND that. Often times, we try something, quit, and try something else. We ease in or jump into something yet not let go of the other thing that drags us down. While in the Cloud of Ambiguity, we look at this or that but may not look at how things can be integrated. Or we make a decision (this or that) and forget about the *and*. What comes after that decision? What is the next step?

Let's take a look at losing weight. We suddenly want to start a new exercise regime, but rarely look at all of the incremental things that we can do to live a healthier lifestyle. It's either drink sugared beverages or not. What if you drank one less sugared beverage a day or a week?

One day at lunch, a colleague was introduced to the "and" concept and it prompted him to think of one thing he could do to live a healthier lifestyle. He mentioned that he had a cabinet full of vitamins. He committed to take one vitamin a day to start living his healthier lifestyle. As he put his hand to his head, it was as if he had a revelation. He exclaimed, "This seems so easy! This *and* that." He was amazed at the simplicity of the solution but hadn't considered it. While he thought about other things he could do to live a healthier lifestyle, he realized that he didn't have to jump immediately into a 1-hour a day workout routine. He just needed to take one step each day to live a healthier lifestyle. He committed to work out on the treadmill for 10 minutes a day. In 365 days, he made incremental changes to his lifestyle.

How often do we make something so complicated when it is as simple as a three letter word: a—n—d?

A health care administrator looked at the *and* concept in her life. She was married and spent more and more time in her job than with her family, which was most important to her. Unfortunately, she was consumed with her career and left little time or energy for what was really important in her life: her husband and her little girl. She was introduced to a home products business. She began to take steps to grow her business. Her little girl began to be her helper in this business and it gave them time together since she operated it from home.

She continued with her full-time Administrator position. Her co-workers would make fun of her as she was creating her side business (the "and" concept). Not only did she spend time with her little girl, but she spent less time on the home products business than her job but made as much income as she did as an Administrator.

While she never expected that the business would be

so profitable, she walked into the organization one day and announced her resignation to continue her home-based business. She was excited in her work and the flexible environment improved her work life balance. She spent time on what was most important to her. She also realized that she enjoyed the support that she received from the other people involved in the home products business.

If she never thought of this *and* that, she never would have pursued the opportunity in her spare time and wouldn't have had another income stream.

That income stream came in handy for another woman who was also in a similar situation. She had a six figure income and found she was stressed nearly every waking moment working in a chaotic environment. When her division was selling off lines of business, she knew that a continued focus on her side business of selling vitamins may turn into a full-time option. When her position was eliminated, she walked away thankful she now could transition to work on the *and* part of her life and had another income stream.

Self-Reflection Moment

Is there a situation in your life where alternatives don't look or seem possible?

What is your "this *and* that?"

What would happen if one income stream was eliminated?

Can you incorporate a this-and-that approach to your life? If so, what is it?

Is there one small step you can take to move beyond where you are today and closer to where you want to be?

Are there two activities that would compliment each other and make life easier for you?

Do you need to balance this *and* that?

Is there something stopping you from looking at this and that?

PHASE 3:

CREATING NEW PATHS

CHAPTER NINETEEN

MOVING FORWARD IN CHANGING TIMES

In Phase 1, Understanding What Motivates You, you created awareness of how you are naturally motivated. It is critical to identify how you got to your place in time. You may have seen a bit of yourself in one or a few of the characters and the way they have navigated through their change based on what motivated them.

Phase 2, Finding Possibilities, introduced you to new concepts and alternative viewpoints while navigating life's changes. You begin to consider previously unconsidered alternatives and learn to create a new future.

As you accept that change will always occur in your life time, it is important to take purposeful action. Purposeful action is that action which aligns with your values, your needs and your vision. Your vision becomes the filter and gauge in life.

Phase 3, Creating New Paths, begins to clear your cloud. You uncover certain values you want to make more dominant in your life.

On your map to being *who* you are, you discover more of what being and living who you are really means. Are you ready to move ahead by doing things differently to maximize your innate motivators?

Recognize that everyone's approach to navigate through change will be different. These next chapters may help you:

- Become focused by taking action that is consistent with your vision not your safety zone.

- Use active listening to manage your inner critic.

- Learn to listen more effectively by layering.

- Use journaling to see where patterns emerge and identify how you can break old patterns so that new opportunities emerge.

- Implement Purpose Points when your safety zones or innate motivators get in the way. (See Chapter 23 for more information.)

Why is it important to align purposeful action as you move ahead?

When you create awareness about the natural way you are motivated *and* manage that which seems so natural to get different results, you produce a sense of confidence and wisdom about your path. Just as important, your vision for your future needs to demonstrate the values of the world or place you want to live in.

You must believe that you have the power to navigate change, to create a life you want to live, and to maximize your fullest authentic potential.

CHAPTER TWENTY

VISION DEVELOPMENT

Our innate motivators drive us through life, yet we need to create an awareness of when they work and when they inhibit our authenticity. When we maximize our natural motivators, create an awareness of them, manage them, and are open to alternatives, we can better navigate significant change. Critical to navigating change is to identify where you are on the map so that you can determine where you want to go.

You have to ask yourself, where am I going? What world do I want to create? What is important? This is where a life vision can guide you in your journey.

People who commit to their life vision realize that they must change their actions and/or behaviors in order to reach that place. They absorb their vision at a level where it changes their actions and the way they think about things. They begin to focus on the world they chose to create. More awareness generates and they listen to the inner voice not the inner critic.

We want to have instant results in life but we need to cultivate our awareness that leads us to it. The more you emerge your awareness of *who* you are and live in alignment with your values, the more you will feel a sense of hope and confidence. Your emerging awareness guides you where your path leads.

Jamie felt stuck in her corporate position. Her job became routine and Jamie was naturally motivated to have variety in her work and needed, in fact, was energized by, people and social contact. She worked alone doing a lot of routine work, which lacked that people contact and the variety in her work she innately needed. But there was something more. She also didn't have the family life she so dreamed of. She found it hard to balance her professional life and her personal life. She did not focus on that which she found most important: her family. While she was a valued employee, she was not living her vision.

She began to write down her vision, who was included in it, and what it looked like. She drew a picture of all of the people in her vision for her future.

She wrote down her values. Balance, to her, was a value. Something she wanted to have happen. And so began her statement for her future that included her value of balance. She posted her vision statement and visual pictures of her future everywhere. It became the future world she wanted to live in. On a daily basis, she said aloud what she wanted in her future, and an interesting thing happened. She began to keep that statement in mind when scheduling her calendar. Instead of saying, "I have no time," she said, "I can't do that this week, but my first availability is next week." She scheduled time for herself and her family. She took control of her schedule rather than her schedule controlling her.

Below is an example of a vision statement:

My Life's Vision is in a place/world that

- embraces *quality*,
- nurtures *wisdom*, and
- values *integrity*.

It is a place/world where we:

- share *uniqueness*
- motivate others
- strive for *excellence*
- and demonstrate *courage, character*, and *balance*.

Can you see what values are important? You will want to make your vision as active and meaningful to you as possible so each value should be accompanied by an action verb (i.e., share, motivate, strive, demonstrate.) What do you think is important for this person? Quality, wisdom, integrity, uniqueness, and balance are all values important to this person.

Your vision will become a filter by which you can make decisions. For example, Jamie was offered an opportunity to take a job out of state with her current employer or find another job. Where does Jamie start with a decision like that? With her vision statement.

Her vision becomes a foundation, especially when unexpected situations occur. Would this new opportunity provide balance? Would it nurture wisdom? Does it affect more than her? How does this opportunity stack up with what the rest of the family wants?

It acts as a filter for the life she wants to create and

keeps decisions in alignment with the vision...that world she wants to create or the environment she wants to live. Likewise, she creates an awareness of how she is naturally motivated and whether she is in the environment that aligns with how she is motivated. This vision for her future is another tool to help her in her journey through life.

Your vision not only becomes the future place you desire to live, but it becomes a foundation for your life's decisions.

SELF-REFLECTION MOMENT

Everyone values something different. Let's start with your values. Following is a list of core values. Select the top twenty. Out of the top twenty, select the ten most important.

Of those ten, select three that are most important. Add any value not already listed, if it is important to you.

Achievement	Affiliation
Artistic Creativity	Adventure
Affection	Arts
Advancement and Promotion	Authenticity
Autonomy/Independence	Authority
Balance	Belonging
Change and Variety	Character
Community	Creativity
Challenge	Compassion
Close Relationships	Competence
Competition	Cooperation
Excitement	Family
Fast Pace	Friendships
Global Focus	Harmony
Impact Society	Influence People
Intellectual Status	Knowledge
Legacy	Location
Love	Minimize Stress
Mobility	Physical Challenge
Power and Authority	Precision Work
Prestige	Profit
Public Contact	Pure Challenge
Recognition	Risk
Security	Stability
Supervision	Time Freedom

Travel	Work Alone
Work Under Pressure	Work With Others
Ecological Awareness	Economic Security
Effectiveness	Ethical Practice/Ethics
Health	Excellence
Excitement	Expertise
Faith	Fame
Fidelity	Financial Gain
Financial Independence	Freedom
Growth	Family
Helping other people	Helping society
Honesty	Independence
Inner Harmony	Integrity
Intellectual Status	Involvement
Job Tranquility	Knowledge
Leadership	Loyalty
Market position	Merit
Meaningful Work	Money
Nature	Order
Personal	Pleasure
Privacy	Public service
Purity	Quality
Respect from others	Religion
Reputation	Responsibility
Security	Self-respect

Serenity   Stability

Service to Others   Sophistication

Spirituality   Status

Supervising Others   Tranquility

Trust   Truth

Uniqueness   Variety

Wealth   Wisdom

Using your selected values, create a statement that reflects your vision for your future. It should be short enough to memorize. It should reflect your personal values and inspire both you and others.

Begin the statement with:

My Life's Vision is a place/world that

(insert action verb) value

(insert action verb) value; and

(insert action verb) value

A place/world where

(include others, people, we, together)

(insert action verb) value

(insert action verb) value and

(insert action verb) value.

Some other action verbs that place your values in action may include:

produces	enables	cultivates	encourages
maximizes	nurtures	expresses	fosters
identifies	creates		

Chapter Twenty-One

Taming the Inner Critic

How do you navigate toward your vision and create more openings to achieve that vision of your future? You may need to be in the moment and tame your inner critic—that part of you that places limitations on your thinking. The inner critic is present in everyone and it emerges when thinking of possibilities, navigating change, and communicating your daily conversations.

This next tool is helpful to master relationships and to give your inner critic another focus. The next time you have a conversation, listen. Really listen without your agenda, persuasion, or judgment. How many people in your life say, "You never listen to me" or "You don't hear me." Because you want to get your agenda, you only hear that which supports your idea or agenda. That is not in-the-moment listening and prevents you from listening to another person's ideas.

One day, Carley made a commitment to herself to really listen to her daughter. No agenda, no judgment, just listen and ask questions to seek understanding.

She needed to be completely focused on her daughter's thoughts and ideas. She realized after the conversation how difficult it was to be fully present with her daughter's ideas. Yet, she decided to take a tool she learned: in-the-moment listening. By practicing in-the-moment listening, she met her daughter where the daughter was in her learning journey. Carley learned how to have a meaningful and enriching conversation through this listening technique.

Later, her daughter commented how nice the conversation was to her. It was not what Carley could tell her daughter, rather the daughter's expressions of her own thoughts and ideas. If only for that moment, Carley had learned to tame her inner critic.

Exercising the Inner Critic

The next time the inner or outer critic is present, try this in-the-moment exercise. During your next conversation, try the following:

1. Ask open-ended questions. Open-ended questions are asked without judgment. You can start by asking:

- What can you tell me about ____?

- What is your business like? How was school? What went well?

- What is possible?

2. While listening, also use another tool: layering. This tool allows you to take a portion of what a person has said and use it in the next open-ended question. The layering technique is especially useful in times of disagreement. When you find yourself layering a conversation, it demands you listen to what the other person says and use what they have said to ask the next open-ended question.

It might look something like this:

Responder: "This report you wrote stinks!"

You: "What about the report do you not like?" (Open-ended question)

Responder: "It doesn't contain an Executive Summary and the points are not concise."

You: "The report should include a summary and main points should be tightened. (rephrased but layered). What are some other changes you might suggest?" (another open-ended question).

Responder: "I don't have any other changes."

You: "What about the report did you like?"

Responder: "I liked the analysis part."

You: "What about the analysis part did you find helpful?"

Responder: "Where we are going to save $1 million if we take advantage of our size."

This technique takes time and work especially if you're in a discussion when emotion runs high or it is a viewpoint that is different than how you see it. When you are focused on layering what the person is saying, it helps take the emotion out of a situation and helps you to focus on the problem.

While using these tools, observe your inner voice. What is the inner critic saying? How is the outer critic present? Is there judgment? Do you want to prove an idea *you* have or are you in the moment with *that* person's idea/feelings? Are you trying to talk or solve a problem *for* them? Do you already formulate what to say next before the other person is finished? Do you ask a leading question in order to close a sale or to preserve your agenda? If the answer is yes, then you are not practicing the in-the-moment listening and your agenda or viewpoint has emerged.

3. Use closed-ended statement to confirm facts.

During the conversation, there may be a time where you need to confirm facts through a closed-ended statement. The closed-ended statement often confirms your understanding or tests your assumption of what you may have heard. It allows the other person to confirm if they have been heard or if you are on the same page.

For example, you attend a meeting and the project manager begins with the status of the project. You think but are unsure of the purpose of the meeting. To confirm your assessment about the purpose of the meeting, you might say, "So, if I understand you correctly, the purpose of this meeting is to determine where we stand in the project."

These in-the-moment listening techniques allows several things to happen:

- ***Helps nurture relationships.***

When using in-the-moment listening, the other person feels listened to and, when they feel heard, they often

144

feel valued. When you are in the moment and focused on what the person said rather than judging, it doesn't give the inner critic an in to your conversation.

When we feel someone has an opposing view, we might call them a name or otherwise negate their viewpoint and move on. Instead, ask yourself, What is good or valuable about what that person said? What is of value in their feedback? Active listening tools help you to understand the other person's viewpoint. It also helps to test your assumptions about what you think the other person is trying to say to you.

How often have you made assumptions and walked away without resolving the issue, or kept that assumption hidden without addressing it?

- *Gives Perspective*

Like other tools, these in-the-moment listening tools help us communicate with a wide-variety of people who simply give and receive information differently than ourselves.

These tools might feel awkward at first, but what emerges during the conversation can be interesting. There are other dynamics involved. If you have typically operated with an outer critic (your inner critic emerging on the outside), that is, frequently communicate what people are doing wrong and criticize others, you may have to build trust first. Trust needs to be restored in time by utilizing the layering tool regularly. People might think you are trying to prove a point or get your agenda across or ask questions to find fault. It would be important if this is the case, to let them know that you are committed to changing the environment and are committed to new listening techniques.

If you typically communicate your ideas frequently, people might wonder why you ask questions instead of talking or persuading. If you generally are quiet and introspective, you may be perceived as unduly inquisitive. Share with them your desire to improve your listening and communication skills and be open when they hold you accountable.

SELF-REFLECTION MOMENT

Think of a time when you were hard on yourself where your inner critic was present. What did your inner critic say to you?

Are you waiting for the perfect opportunity?

Is waiting for the perfect opportunity a way for you to avoid something?

Does your inner critic say that you need to get results?

Does your inner critic push you for acceptance by others?

Does your inner critic cause you to rush to judgment, conclusions or critique something or someone?

When and how can you use this tool?

Chapter Twenty-Two

Journal on the Journey

Thus far, you may have created a new awareness of your natural needs and motivators. The secret to discovering your talents, how you navigate through your Cloud of Ambiguity (or change), and the possibilities to achieve the vision for your future is to understand the unique way you and others are motivated and how to manage those motivators. You may have been able to identify what's important through one or more of the characters featured. You may have learned that letting go of what you did or an event of what happened can lead you on your path to move ahead. Your timeline may have helped you to see when key changes occur in your life to date.

These are all secrets that help you to navigate and embrace change. But how can you prepare for changes and create perspective on change?

Journaling provides reflection time and records when you are aligning yourself with your vision. You may see key messages as you go through past changes, and more importantly, it helps you to focus on aligning action you take with your vision.

In journaling, it is important to focus on what you can be grateful for and the positive attributes of transition. A caustic inner critic can keep you focused on the negative and that could be present in your journal. You want the journal to have a balance of gratitude and to let go of what no longer works.

Sandy experienced several life transitions and, each time, what was important to her evolved, just as Sandy had evolved as an individual in a perfect order. It wasn't until she re-read her journal of those events that she realized why those changes had occurred. She learned: learned about her life, who she was becoming, and the future she wanted to create for herself.

She wrote a few lines about what happened each day or week, her hopes, her dreams, and her vision. This journal served as a reminder of her achievements, a focus on what she wanted to have happen for her future, and simply an outlet for those events that got her down.

For Sandy, the process of journaling helped her move *forward* through change. It can be helpful to journal experiences, results, new thoughts or new ways of doing things or approaching relationships.

SELF-REFLECTION MOMENT

If you want to change behaviors you learned, be honest with yourself. Reflect on how you could have done things differently. Celebrate what you did well.

While journaling, ask:

Did you use layering and open-ended questions with your family, teenager or co-worker?

How could you have handled a situation differently and without judgment?

What was valuable about what the other person said?

What key things would you like to place in your journal?

What are your natural needs and/or motivators?

Do you want to commit to journaling?

CHAPTER TWENTY-THREE

PURPOSE POINTS

When a basketball athlete has a ball and wants to advance it, what are his/her choices? If heavily guarded, the athlete might pivot. Pivoting allows the athlete to gain a different perspective and redefine the purpose (advancing the ball to score points) especially when blocked.

Purpose Points are times in life where we need to take a different perspective (to pivot), much like the athlete takes when they take a different perspective on how to get the ball in the basket. Purpose Points allow you to:

- Gain clarity on your purpose.

- View situations differently.

- Move ahead particularly when your safety zone, behaviors, or the natural way you are motivated get in the way.

- Focus on the vision when unplanned events occur.

- Embrace controlled thinking during chaos.

- Give attention to what's really important.

When you need to change the way you look at something, ask yourself:

1. What's really important?

2. What is actually happening or about to happen right now?

3. What am I thinking, feeling and doing right now? Are my natural motivators or things I need getting in the way of a successful resolution or my purpose?

4. What do I want to have happen that will serve my/ the future vision or commitments?

5. What action (or inaction) can I take that supports me to achieve desirable outcomes? What action (or inaction) can I take that supports my vision for my future or my purpose?

The more you use Purpose Points, the more you will make decisions in alignment with your vision and the more you are empowered over your actions. You can use Purpose Points to uncover the alignment between the vision for your life and the vision in the work you do or realize the disconnects.

Self Reflection Moment

What could practicing in-the-moment listening give you?

Is reacting an issue?

What is happening?

How can you use Purpose Points to view an event?

How can you see a situation differently?

What is the purpose of your action or inaction?

CHAPTER TWENTY-FOUR

ACTION PLANNING

By now, you observed the innate way you're motivated and brought awareness to what you need and
want for your future. You may be comfortably uncomfortable at this time. At some point, though, you may
need to take purposeful action to continue to transform
and to reach your desired result or vision.

Action Plan Development helps keep you on track. It
should align your actions with your vision. An action plan
is exemplified below. Each area of your life can have its
own plan. Committing to a starting date can be impera-
tive to building a life you want to live. In addition, many
people start with wanting to lose weight; however, what
they truly want is to be healthier and feel better about
themselves. The Project Name could be called, "Project
Healthy Life" or something that inspires you.

Each positive goal is outlined with corresponding action steps and key successes. Key Successes may include
a tangible result, the amount of time spent with an action or an intangible result (related to how you feel.) Up-
dates are used to ensure you keep on track. Remember

your Vision Statement? That is also part of your plan to ensure that the action is purposeful and in alignment with the plan.

The example below identifies Project Healthy Life.

Project Name: Project Healthy Life (Action Oriented)	Start Date: Today End Date: Ongoing
Overall Result/ Domain More Energy/Health	What you are consciously telling yourself: "I have an abundance of energy." "I am healthy." "I will meet my goals."
Vision Statement My life's vision is…	Responsible Party: Me!

Goal	Action Steps	Key Successes	Update
Increase Exercise	Get on treadmill for 10 minutes for 2 weeks. Treadmill for 15 minutes after 3 weeks.	10 minutes/ daily	

SELF-REFLECTION MOMENT

During Action Plan Development keep these points in mind:

- Are your plans/dates achievable?

- Does it set out to create/do what you need/want?

- How does it align with what's truly important?

- Are there too many plans?

- What are the priority items?

- Is scheduling your time important?

- Can you incorporate activities? (i.e., If your plan is to increase exercise, can you select a parking space further from your building or take the stairs to the office?)

- What may stop you from reaching your desired outcomes personally, professionally, spiritually, in relationships, and in business?

Chapter Twenty-Five

Putting It All Together

An event, for many people, is the catalyst where they introspectively look at who they are and it shifts their path. Shifting the path can be unnerving and confusing especially when it is unexpected or unanticipated. Awareness of your natural motivators and needs helps you to navigate through that ambiguity.

Those motivators can be helping hands or hindrances. Creating an awareness about your needs/motivators, developing a purposeful vision for the future, and keeping focused on your values can keep you attentive to your direction and living in concert with those values. When there are unanticipated events, navigating the change now has a foundation.

As your awareness awakens, a look at your lifeline helps you to see patterns or cycle times: how certain behaviors have worked and not worked for you, and how you learned some lessons or revisit similar events and situations. You may even find intervals where change occurs at certain times in your life and so an event is in the normal course of when change occurs for you.

As humans, we try to have control, whether it is control over ideas or control of a process or making *it* right—whatever *it* is and if there is a *right* way. However, there is power in letting go and having faith that messages will be brought to you to create a path when you can consider the unconsidered and test those assumptions that inhibit your growth.

In my journey, these are the things I've come to know.

- The Cloud of Ambiguity is real for the person experiencing it.

- Embracing *who* you are and your experiences can inspire others to capture their inner strength.

- Navigating through the Cloud of Ambiguity can be heart wrenching and hard.

- Letting go can create peace and hope.

- Living your vision can be difficult, but living without one can be even harder. A vision can lead to your purpose in life.

- Adapting a mindset of faith during transition can be empowering.

- We are all on this earth for a reason. We need to go through what we go through to develop the resilience to be our authentic selves and find our paths in this journey called life.

- Acceptance of where you and other people are in their learning journey and how they are naturally motivated creates empowerment and inner peace.

- We have tools at our disposal to use or not to use…it is a choice.

We make choices every day about what will inspire us and what we will allow to get us down. We have a choice to move ahead or allow ourselves to stay stuck in a rut.

We have the power to let go, the power to hang on and the power to be: be all of who we were designed to be. We have our authentic selves that continue to evolve and emerge each day through every experience. Unlock the secret to navigate change, by uncovering and maximizing the genuine you.

BEGIN WITH A DOWNLOAD!

Continue to develop finding your passage to your purpose. We have made the next step simple and inexpensive. Visit us at www.memyselfandwhy.com to purchase your copy of "Drive Time: Time to Think." Listen to new author, Lisa Mininni, as she guides you through your thought-provoking insights moving from chaos to balanced control.

GET YOUR ORGANIZATION IN GEAR!

Work with the same vision in mind. Purchase the book for your colleagues, corporate retreats, or special occasions, and be the catalyst to get people aligned! Go to www.memyselfandwhy.com.

BRING LISA MININNI TO YOUR ORGANIZATION!

Lisa Mininni is known as an energizing speaker leaving participants with unexpected takeaways. Her invigorating presentations cover the topics of leadership, motivations, and navigating change. In addition to speaking, Lisa is known for her strengths in strategic planning, consulting, professional coaching, team building, and aligning people-positive and bottom line results. Lisa is President of Excellerate Associates, LLC, a consulting, coaching and training firm and Founder of The C Club, for cancer conquerors offering programs to help reclaim, reshape, and renew life. Visit Excellerate Associates' website at www.excellerateassociates.com or The C Club's website at www.theclub.org.